Games and Natural Language Processing (Games & NLP 2022)

Held at LREC 2022

Marseille, France
20 – 25 June 2022

Editor:

Chris Madge

ISBN: 978-1-7138-6121-8

Printed from e-media with permission by:

Curran Associates, Inc.
57 Morehouse Lane
Red Hook, NY 12571

Some format issues inherent in the e-media version may also appear in this print version.

Association for Computational Linguistics
209 N. Eighth Street
Stroudsburg, Pennsylvania 18360

Phone: 1-570-476-8006
Fax: 1-570-476-0860

acl@aclweb.org

Additional copies of this publication are available from:

Curran Associates, Inc.
57 Morehouse Lane
Red Hook, NY 12571 USA
Phone: 845-758-0400
Fax: 845-758-2633
Email: curran@proceedings.com
Web: www.proceedings.com

LREC 2022 Workshop
Language Resources and Evaluation Conference
20-25 June 2022

**Games and Natural Language Processing
(Games & NLP 2022)**

PROCEEDINGS

Editor:
Chris Madge

Proceedings of the LREC 2022 workshop on Games and Natural Language Processing (Games & NLP 2022)

Edited by:
Chris Madge

For more information:
European Language Resources Association (ELRA)
9 rue des Cordeli‘eres
75013, Paris
France
http://www.elra.info
Email: lrec@elda.org

Message from the General Chair

This volume documents the Proceedings of the Games and Natural Language Processing Workshop, held on (25th June 2022) as part of the LREC 2022 conference (International Conference on Language Resources and Evaluation).

This workshop examines the use of games and gamification for Natural Language Processing (NLP) tasks, as well as how NLP research can advance player engagement and communication within games. The Games and NLP workshop aims to promote and explore the possibilities for research and practical applications of games and gamification that have a core NLP aspect, either to generate resources and perform language tasks or as a game mechanic itself. This workshop investigates computational and theoretical aspects of natural language research that would be beneficial for designing and building novel game experiences, or for processing texts to conduct formal game studies. NLP would benefit from games in obtaining language resources (e.g., construction of a thesaurus or a parser through a crowdsourcing game), or in learning the linguistic characteristics of game users as compared to those of other domains.

Workshop website: https://gamesandnlp.com

Organizers

Chris Madge, chair (Queen Mary University of London)
Jon Chamberlain (University of Essex, UK)
Karën Fort (Sorbonne Université, France)
Udo Kruschwitz (University of Regensburg, Germany)
Stephanie Lukin (U.S. Army Research Laboratory)

Program Committee:

Alice Millour (Sorbonne Université)
Andrew Gordon (University of Southern California, Institute of Creative Technology)
Andrew Stern (Playabl Studios, US)
Chris Cieri (Linguistic Data Consortium, University of Pennsylvania, US)
Ian Horswill (Northwestern University)
James Fiumara (Linguistic Data Consortium, University of Pennsylvania, US)
Jonathan Lessard (Universite Condoria)
Josh Miller (Northeastern University, US)
Mariët Theune (University of Twente)
Massimo Poesio (Queen Mary University Of London)
Mathieu Lafourcade (LIRMM, France)
Melissa Roemmele (SDL, US)
Morteza Behrooz (University of California, Santa Cruz, US)
Paulo Gomes (Samsung Research America)
Pedro Santos (INESC-ID & Instituto Superior Técnico, University of Lisbon)
Richard Bartle (University of Essex, UK)
Seth Cooper (Northeastern University, US)
Valerio Basile (University of Turin, Italy)
Verena Lyding (EURAC, Italy)
Wookhee Min (North Carolina State University)
Luis Morgado da Costa (Nanyang Technological University, Singapore)
Timothee Mickus (Université de Lorraine)

Table of Contents

Workshop Program

Saturday 25 June 2022

14:40–15:00 *An Analysis of Abusive Language Data Collected through a Game with a Purpose*
Federico Bonetti and Sara Tonelli

15:00–15:20 *Applying Gamification Incentives in the Revita Language-learning System*
Jue Hou, Ilmari Kylliäinen, Anisia Katinskaia, Giacomo Furlan and Roman Yangarber

15:20–15:40 *Less Text, More Visuals: Evaluating the Onboarding Phase in a GWAP for NLP*
Fatima Althani, Chris Madge and Massimo Poesio

15:40–16:00 *NLU for Game-based Learning in Real: Initial Evaluations*
Eda Okur, Saurav Sahay and Lama Nachman

17:00–17:20 *How NLP Can Strengthen Digital Game Based Language Learning Resources for Less Resourced Languages*
Monica Ward, Liang Xu and Elaine Uí Dhonnchadha

17:20–17:40 *The "Actors Challenge" Project: Collecting Data on Intonation Profiles via a Web Game*
Natallia Chaiko, Sia Sepanta and Roberto Zamparelli

17:40–18:00 *Generating Descriptive and Rules-Adhering Spells for Dungeons & Dragons Fifth Edition*
Pax Newman and Yudong Liu

Proceedings of the 9th Games and Natural Language Processing Workshop @LREC2022, pages 1–6
Marseille, 25 June 2022

An Analysis of Abusive Language Data Collected through a Game with a Purpose

Federico Bonetti[1,2], Sara Tonelli[1]
[1]Fondazione Bruno Kessler, Trento, Italy, [2]University of Trento, Italy
{fbonetti, satonelli}@fbk.eu

Abstract

In this work we present an analysis of abusive language annotations collected through a 3D video game. With this approach, we are able to involve in the annotation teenagers, i.e. typical targets of cyberbullying, whose data are usually not available for research purposes. Using the game in the framework of educational activities to empower teenagers against online abuse we are able to obtain insights into how teenagers communicate, and what kind of messages they consider more offensive. While players produced interesting annotations and the distributions of classes between players and experts are similar, we obtained a significant number of mismatching judgements between experts and players.

Keywords: game with a purpose, linguistic annotation, offensive language

1. Introduction

Cyberbullying has been recognised as a major public health issue, which can lead to severe negative consequences for teenagers, from self-harm to suicide (Tokunaga, 2010; Kowalski et al., 2014). Nevertheless, cyberbullying attacks are frequent in private chats and channels, while only a small fraction of them is visible in public accounts. This makes it hard to study the behaviour of adolescents online, since data collection from major social media platforms is strictly limited. The few existing works dealing with NLP and cyberbullying resort to simulations (Sprugnoli et al., 2018; Menini et al., 2020), create datasets starting from school bulletin boards (Nitta et al., 2013) or extract posts from the few available online sources like ask.fm (Hee et al., 2015; Safi Samghabadi et al., 2020; Rathnayake et al., 2020), where however users are anonymous and it is not possible to identify teenagers among them.

Collecting reliable data, while respecting teenagers' privacy, is therefore of paramount importance to study cyberbullying phenomena. Novel ways to understand the behaviour of teenagers with respect to verbal abuse online are needed. Past works have proposed to use video games to empower teenagers in countering cyberbullying and increase their resilience (Calvo-Morata et al., 2019). In this work we employ *High School Superhero* (HSS) (Bonetti and Tonelli, 2021a) as a tool to involve teenagers, i.e. typical targets of cyberbullying, in a game where the main goal is to decrease the amount of offensive language used in a small town. The players have the possibility to critically evaluate potentially offensive sentences and make them not offensive. As a side effect, the game allows the collection of a large number of sentences judged by teenagers in the form of a gamified crowd-sourced task. Thus, playing with HSS can also lead to the creation of linguistic annotated datasets for abusive language detection. We focus this contribution on the analysis of the annotated data and the challenges of using HSS to collect abusive language annotations.

2. Related work

In NLP, several games with a purpose (GWAPs) have been proposed in the past to address different linguistic tasks: *Phrase Detectives* (Poesio et al., 2013) for anaphora resolution; *OnToGalaxy* (Krause et al., 2010) for semantic linking; *The Knowledge Towers* and *Infection* for validating and extending ontologies (Vannella et al., 2014); *Puzzle Racer* and *KaBoom!* (Jurgens and Navigli, 2014) for sense-image mapping and word sense disambiguation; *WordClicker* (Madge et al., 2019) for Part-of-Speech tagging; *Zombilingo* (Fort et al., 2014) for dependency syntax annotation, and *Wordrobe* (Venhuizen et al., 2013) for word sense labeling. Concerning the use of gamification to raise awareness against cyberbullying, past works showed that increasing empathy is crucial to controlling cyberbullying (Barreda-Ángeles et al., 2021; Del Rey et al., 2016) and games can help in this sense as shown by (Calvo-Morata et al., 2019). They tested *Conectado*, a game where users take the perspective of bullied victims, with school teachers and students aged from 12 to 17. The authors showed that this change of perspective has a positive impact on awareness and empathy, since players can learn more about bullying and what consequences it can have. (DeSmet et al., 2018), on the other hand, stress the importance of promoting positive bystander behavior. In particular, they found that after playing their serious game, participants reported an increase in self-efficacy to end cyberbullying and intention to act as a positive bystander. Using High School Superhero in classes aims to pursue both goals: on the one hand, it should empower teenagers by making them more aware of the language used in online conversations and of their offensive potential. On the

Figure 1: Task mechanic 1 (overhearing dialogues)

Figure 2: Task mechanic 2: Erasing graffiti

other hand, it allows the collection of sentences annotated as offensive or not. In this work, we focus in particular on the second aspect.

3. Design of High School Superhero

In this Section we summarise the main features of High School Superhero (HSS), the 3D game we have used to collect annotations about abusive language.
HSS is a 3D role-playing game set in a small town that allows players to change or erase parts of sentences displayed in different ways. After a character creation screen, players can explore a town to perform the task in dedicated spots. The theme and setting are relevant to the target domain of cyberbullying (Ahmad and Law, 2021). In fact, the very act of explaining to the players who they are within the fictional world (a student specifically chosen to fix the language spoken near and inside a school) and what their goal is in ethical terms (reducing the influence of bullies to save the students) may already foster on its own an appropriate sympathetic response (Belman and Flanagan, 2010; Ryan and Staines, 2016).

3.1. Task mechanics

The game contains 2 different types of activities, so-called *task mechanics* (Bonetti and Tonelli, 2021b). In Task Mechanic 1 (Figure 1), players can listen to conversations happening among non-player characters and see a preview of what they are going to say. In particular, when the player goes near a certain group of students, it is possible to overhear their conversation. Before every message, the player is able to read the speaker's mind: a cloud is shown where tokens are freely modifiable. Whenever a change is made, the student in the group says what the player has told them to say, then they act surprised and look puzzled. Both the modified sentence and the original sentence are kept in order to have examples of abusive sentences and possible fixes. The new sentence can be similar to the original one or rewritten from scratch, since the focus is on knowing if, not how, the sentences have been modified.
In Task Mechanic 2 (Figure 2), players erase graffiti off the ground or walls. Players are instructed to remove graffiti that contain abusive language. Players can erase tokens by using a sponge and a consumable called 'soap'. Words are considered erased when more than 80% of the word surface has been wiped. It is possible to go back and cancel the erasing if needed. This allows to make a new annotation, using additional soap, but it does not grant additional points, otherwise players would be able to spam annotations on the same graffiti to gain points.

3.2. Side mechanics

Side mechanics, in particular mechanics that do not contribute directly to the execution of annotation tasks, are also present. These include:

Collectible elements: Crystals are an in-game currency that can be spent to acquire both power-ups and task-related resources. Collectibles, such as coins, diamonds and the like, have been found to be quite effective in increasing the player's engagement and time spent in video games (Naglé et al., 2021).

Navigation power-ups: The Rocket Boots, a special pair of shoes, allow users to jump as high as some rooftops. An electric scooter allows users to move faster around the town. Lastly, the Glider allows players to jump off buildings and gently glide to the ground.

Quests, a hallmark of role-playing games, are also present. They have been implemented in the form of rather simple missions, where random characters ask the player to erase some graffiti in the area before the time is up.

4. Activity and Data Description

4.1. Activity Setup

The game was administered to selected students in the context of a project aimed at raising awareness on cyberbullying and online abuses targeting teenagers. We carried out in total 6 focus group sessions in 6 Italian middle and high schools. The procedure was approved by the Ethics Advisory Board of the project and of the authors' institution. Before the activities, the participants' parents signed a consent form. Also the participants gave their consent and, before using the game, were reminded that they could quit the activity in any moment.
The procedure was carried out in complete anonymity. Prior to playing, participants were briefed on the activity. They were briefly shown the game and told that it was about abusive language detection: sentences that

they deemed abusive should be corrected (annotated) by erasing words in the case of graffiti and by erasing *or* changing words in the case of dialogue lines. They were also told that they could decide to change or erase only a part of the sentence or no tokens at all, leaving the text unchanged if no offense was detected. This is important as participants may be eager to play and try out the mechanics regardless of the content of messages.

4.2. Data Selection

Since our goal is to analyse the quality of the offensive language dataset collected through the game, we carefully select the sentences to be displayed to the players. We rely on the dataset presented in (Sprugnoli et al., 2018), which contains simulations of cyberbullying interactions collected in classes through a Whatsapp chat. The sentences, in Italian, have been also manually labeled as abusive or not and associated with a category label such as *Body shaming*, *Threat or blackmail*, *Racism*, *Sexism*, *Curse or Exclusion*, *Generic offense*. Using this dataset allows us to compare the judgments collected through the game with the gold labels previously assigned by linguists during manual annotation.
Sentences were divided into different sets according to the target group. Indeed, in some classes we had to be careful not to administer certain types of sentences that could have some people re-experience distressful situations, therefore we followed teachers' suggestions on how to select the data. Sentences with explicit sexual content were always omitted. In general, students from the same class were shown the same sentences, and each class could potentially annotate up to 300 sentences.

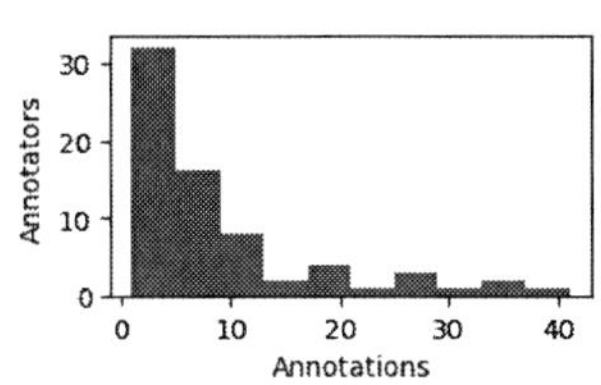

Figure 3: Distribution of annotations per annotator

5. Data Analysis

5.1. Annotation distribution

In total, 590 annotations were collected on 199 sentences from 70 players. The mean number of annotations per participant was 8.42 (SD=9.22); the median was 5; the mode was 2. 50% of participants contributed between 1 and 7 annotations while the top annotator provided as many as 41 annotations. See Figure 3 for a distribution of annotations.
We focus our analysis on the set of annotated sentences for which it is possible to obtain a majority vote, or that were annotated only once. These are overall 162 sentences.

		Players		Tot.
		O	N	
Expert	O	79	34	113
	N	26	23	49
	Tot.	105	57	162

Table 1: Expert judgements vs majority judgements (O=*Offensive*, N=*Not offensive*).

We report in Table 1) the distribution of the collected annotations. We compare them with the annotations from the original dataset, assigned by linguists. Overall, we observe a slight increase of offensive annotations in the dataset by experts. Furthermore, the two sets of annotations match only partially, in particular only 23 sentences were considered not offensive both by experts and players. Expert annotations in this study are shown mainly with the purpose of understanding the degree of mismatch and to observe patterns that differ among the offensive categories. Given the differences between interfaces (only teenagers used the gamified one) and the subjectivity of the task, agreement is not used as an annotation quality metric. For a detailed analysis of mismatches see the following Sections.

5.2. Experts vs. Players' Annotations

We display in Figure 4 the detailed distribution of the labels assigned by Experts (left), compared with the distribution of the labels in the dataset annotated by Players (right). The diagram refers to the 162 sentences analysed in Table 1.

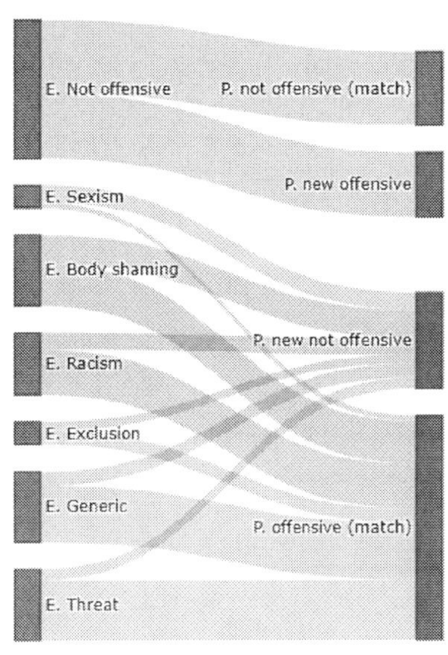

Figure 4: Distribution of the categories in the annotations by Experts (E) (left) and Players (P) (right). Players' annotations marked with *(match)* have the same offensive/not offensive label as in the expert dataset

The figure shows that most of the sentences referring

to specific offensive categories labeled by experts have been recognised as offensive also by players. An interesting exception is the *Sexist* category, whose sentences have been mostly considered not offensive in the game, highlighting the need to raise awareness on misogynistic and sexist language among teenagers. A similar trend exists for the *Body shaming* category, and interestingly during the focus groups students often referred to this category as one of the most important insults to tackle. Also sentences in the *Exclusion* category, which encompasses cases of direct attacks aimed at detaching the counterpart from social relations such as "shut up" and "go away", have been considered not offensive in some cases.

In general, players tended to tag sentences as *not offensive* more frequently than linguists. The mismatching sentences could be due to differences in perception between the two groups of annotators or to considering sentences in a dialogue context (see Section 5.3). It is likely that linguists, who originally annotated the dialogue turns, focused more on the single utterances without considering much the thread context. This would confirm also the findings in (Menini et al., 2021), showing that sentences are less likely to be labeled as offensive when annotators consider the discourse context. However, it should be noted that *P. new offensive* sentences could be caused also by a certain eagerness to try out the game and its mechanics, while *P. new not offensive* sentences could be caused by not paying attention or accidental skipping. To partially solve this problem, however, we let players skip dialogue sentences only after 1 second from the onset.

5.3. Qualitative Analysis

One legitimate concern is that, when changing sentences, players could write something even more offensive just to have fun. However, students seem to have gone by the guidelines. For example, *You butterball you're really fat, yesterday I saw you on the guinness world records as the fattest person alive* ('Palla di lardo sei proprio un ciccione ieri ti ho visto sul guinness world records per il più grasso al mondo') was changed to *You **forkball** you're really **beautiful** yesterday I saw you on the guinness world records as the **most beautiful** person alive.* Although 'fork' does not really make sense, it still does not make the sentence offensive, and therefore it does not go against the purpose of keeping pairs of negative and positive/neutral examples. Regarding similar examples with other sentences, in sentence *You don't know? Haha, what a loser*, 'loser' was changed to '**good person**'.

Concerning the graffiti, sentence *Indeed, you horrid nerd* ('Appunto, secchiona orribile') was changed to *Indeed you ~~horrid~~ nerd* by one participant, to *Indeed you ~~horrid nerd~~* by another and lastly it was erased completely by another still. It looks like participants preferred to erase the whole sentence rather than offensive words or random words. For example, *It was always your fault!* ('È sempre stata colpa tua!') was erased completely by 3 users. One changed it to *It was always ~~your~~ fault.* The reference to the victim was erased, which is acceptable in the context of neutralizing offenses.

Regarding sentences originally labeled as *Not offensive* that were annotated as *Offensive* by players, consider this sentence, which is in the *P. new offensive* category: *At least I have intelligence* ('Almeno ho l'intelligenza'). This may not be offensive in the sense that it is not overtly offensive per se. It could imply two different things: that the person who utters the sentence has many flaws except stupidity; or that the counterpart is not intelligent. It is possible that players interpreted it according to its most hateful meaning, also because of the context of the dialogue and the focus group activity, where they could have acted like they were being tested on their readiness to spot offensive language. Distributing the game 'in the wild', with a written tutorial modified according to the first feedback described in this paper, may yield different results.

Interestingly, in *It's true he did not cause the team to lose, he caused it to be disqualified* ('È vero non ha fatto perdere la squadra, la ha fatta squalificare'), 'be disqualified' was changed to '**qualify**' by one participant and to '**win**' by another. These annotations are particularly worth examining, since the sentence is not overtly offensive, as it does not contain any specific insult; however, it may imply that whoever caused the team to be disqualified deserves hate or contempt. Through HSS it seems possible to retrieve judgements that come from reasoning about the background of a given utterance, given that a certain number of sentences in a sequence refer to the same topic or situation.

6. Conclusion

In this work we have presented an analysis of the annotations collected through the 3D game with a purpose "High School Superhero" on a cyberbullying dataset. The game was deployed in the context of focus groups held with 6 Italian classes of students. We gathered in total 590 annotations from 70 participants.

We observed considerable mismatch between annotations by linguists and those collected through the game. This might be due to differences in the perception of the offenses by the two different groups of annotators or to behaviour caused by the game, such as accidental skipping (which however regarded the dialogues alone, and which was curbed by a quality control step) or eagerness to change the sentences. We plan to counter this last problem in the future by making annotation of non-offensive sentences more rewarding. The findings of this paper need however to be confirmed by further research, one limitation being the small sample size. Another aspect worth exploring in the future is a qualitative analysis of players' behaviour based on post-hoc questionnaires. This would shed more light on why annotators annotated as they did.

7. Acknowledgements

We thank all participants that played with the game to annotate the dataset. Part of this work has been funded by the KID_ACTIONS REC-AG project (n. 101005518) on "Kick-off preventIng and responDing to children and AdolesCenT cyberbullyIng through innovative mOnitoring and educatioNal technologieS".

8. Bibliographical References

Ahmad, A. and Law, E. L.-C. (2021). Educators as Gamemasters: Creating Serious Role Playing Game with. *Proceedings of the ACM on Human-Computer Interaction*, 5(CHI PLAY):1–29, October.

Barreda-Ángeles, M., Serra-Blasco, M., Trepat, E., Pereda-Baños, A., Pàmias, M., Palao, D., Goldberg, X., and Cardoner, N. (2021). Development and experimental validation of a dataset of 360°-videos for facilitating school-based bullying prevention programs. *Computers & Education*, 161:104065.

Belman, J. and Flanagan, M. (2010). Designing Games to Foster Empathy. 14(2):11.

Bonetti, F. and Tonelli, S. (2021a). Challenges in designing games with a purpose for abusive language annotation. In *Proceedings of the First Workshop on Bridging Human–Computer Interaction and Natural Language Processing*, pages 60–65, Online, April. Association for Computational Linguistics.

Bonetti, F. and Tonelli, S. (2021b). Measuring orthogonal mechanics in linguistic annotation games. *Proc. ACM Hum. Comput. Interact.*, 5(CHI):1–16.

Calvo-Morata, A., Freire-Moran, M., Martinez-Ortiz, I., and Fernandez-Manjon, B. (2019). Applicability of a Cyberbullying Videogame as a Teacher Tool: Comparing Teachers and Educational Sciences Students. *IEEE Access*, 7:55841–55850.

Del Rey, R., Lazuras, L., Casas, J. A., Barkoukis, V., Ortega-Ruiz, R., and Tsorbatzoudis, H. (2016). Does empathy predict (cyber) bullying perpetration, and how do age, gender and nationality affect this relationship? *Learning and Individual Differences*, 45:275–281, January.

DeSmet, A., Bastiaensens, S., Cleemput, K. V., Poels, K., Vandebosch, H., Deboutte, G., Herrewijn, L., Malliet, S., Pabian, S., Broeckhoven, F. V., Troyer, O. D., Deglorie, G., Hoecke, S. V., Samyn, K., and Bourdeaudhuij, I. D. (2018). The efficacy of the Friendly Attac serious digital game to promote prosocial bystander behavior in cyberbullying among young adolescents: A cluster-randomized controlled trial. *Computers in Human Behavior*, 78:336 – 347.

Fort, K., Guillaume, B., and Chastant, H. (2014). Creating *Zombilingo* , a game with a purpose for dependency syntax annotation. In *Proceedings of the First International Workshop on Gamification for Information Retrieval - GamifIR '14*, pages 2–6, Amsterdam, The Netherlands. ACM Press.

Hee, C. V., Lefever, E., Verhoeven, B., Mennes, J., Desmet, B., Pauw, G. D., Daelemans, W., and Hoste, V. (2015). Detection and fine-grained classification of cyberbullying events. In Galia Angelova, et al., editors, *Recent Advances in Natural Language Processing, RANLP 2015, 7-9 September, 2015, Hissar, Bulgaria*, pages 672–680. RANLP 2015 Organising Committee / ACL.

Jurgens, D. and Navigli, R. (2014). It's All Fun and Games until Someone Annotates: Video Games with a Purpose for Linguistic Annotation. *Transactions of the Association for Computational Linguistics*, 2:449–464, December.

Kowalski, R. M., Giumetti, G. W., Schroeder, A., and Lattanner, M. R. (2014). Bullying in the digital age: a critical review and meta-analysis of cyberbullying research among youth. *Psychological bulletin*, 140 4:1073–137.

Krause, M., Takhtamysheva, A., Wittstock, M., and Malaka, R. (2010). Frontiers of a paradigm: exploring human computation with digital games. In *Proceedings of the ACM SIGKDD Workshop on Human Computation - HCOMP '10*, pages 22–25, Washington DC. ACM Press.

Madge, C., Bartle, R., Chamberlain, J., Kruschwitz, U., and Poesio, M. (2019). Incremental Game Mechanics Applied to Text Annotation. In *Proceedings of the Annual Symposium on Computer-Human Interaction in Play*, pages 545–558, Barcelona Spain, October. ACM.

Menini, S., Aprosio, A. P., and Tonelli, S. (2020). A multimodal dataset of images and text to study abusive language. In Johanna Monti, et al., editors, *Proceedings of the Seventh Italian Conference on Computational Linguistics, CLiC-it 2020, Bologna, Italy, March 1-3, 2021*, volume 2769 of *CEUR Workshop Proceedings*. CEUR-WS.org.

Menini, S., Aprosio, A. P., and Tonelli, S. (2021). Abuse is contextual, what about nlp? the role of context in abusive language annotation and detection. *arXiv preprint arXiv:2103.14916*.

Naglé, T., Bateman, S., and Birk, M. V. (2021). Pathfinder: The Behavioural and Motivational Effects of Collectibles in Gamified Software Training. *Proceedings of the ACM on Human-Computer Interaction*, 5(CHI PLAY):1–23, October.

Nitta, T., Masui, F., Ptaszynski, M., Kimura, Y., Rzepka, R., and Araki, K. (2013). Detecting cyberbullying entries on informal school websites based on category relevance maximization. In *Proceedings of the Sixth International Joint Conference on Natural Language Processing*, pages 579–586, Nagoya, Japan, October. Asian Federation of Natural Language Processing.

Poesio, M., Chamberlain, J., Kruschwitz, U., Robaldo, L., and Ducceschi, L. (2013). Phrase detectives: Utilizing collective intelligence for internet-scale language resource creation. *ACM Transactions on*

Interactive Intelligent Systems, 3(1):1–44, April.

Rathnayake, G., Atapattu, T., Herath, M., Zhang, G., and Falkner, K. (2020). Enhancing the identification of cyberbullying through participant roles. In *Proceedings of the Fourth Workshop on Online Abuse and Harms*, pages 89–94, Online, November. Association for Computational Linguistics.

Ryan, M. and Staines, D. (2016). Four Lenses for Designing Morally Engaging Games. page 16.

Safi Samghabadi, N., López Monroy, A. P., and Solorio, T. (2020). Detecting early signs of cyberbullying in social media. In *Proceedings of the Second Workshop on Trolling, Aggression and Cyberbullying*, pages 144–149, Marseille, France, May. European Language Resources Association (ELRA).

Sprugnoli, R., Menini, S., Tonelli, S., Oncini, F., and Piras, E. (2018). Creating a WhatsApp Dataset to Study Pre-teen Cyberbullying. In *Proceedings of the 2nd Workshop on Abusive Language Online (ALW2)*, pages 51–59, Brussels, Belgium. Association for Computational Linguistics.

Tokunaga, R. S. (2010). Following you home from school: A critical review and synthesis of research on cyberbullying victimization. *Computers in Human Behavior*, 26(3):277 – 287.

Vannella, D., Jurgens, D., Scarfini, D., Toscani, D., and Navigli, R. (2014). Validating and Extending Semantic Knowledge Bases using Video Games with a Purpose. In *Proceedings of the 52nd Annual Meeting of the Association for Computational Linguistics (Volume 1: Long Papers)*, pages 1294–1304, Baltimore, Maryland. Association for Computational Linguistics.

Venhuizen, N. J., Evang, K., Basile, V., and Bos, J. (2013). Gamification for Word Sense Labeling. In *Proceedings of the International Conference on Computational Semantics (IWCS)*, pages 397–403.

Proceedings of the 9th Games and Natural Language Processing Workshop @LREC2022, pages 7–16
Marseille, 25 June 2022

Applying gamification incentives in the Revita language-learning system

Jue Hou[1], Ilmari Kylliäinen[2], Anisia Katinskaia[1], Giacomo Furlan[1] and Roman Yangarber[2]
[1]Department of Computer Science
[2]Department of Digital Humanities
University of Helsinki
{firstname.lastname}@helsinki.fi

Abstract

We explore the importance of gamification features in a language-learning platform designed for intermediate-to-advanced learners. Our main thesis is: learning toward advanced levels requires a massive investment of time. If the learner engages in more practice sessions, and if the practice sessions are longer, we can expect the results to be better. This principle appears to be tautologically self-evident. Yet, keeping the learner engaged in general—and building gamification features in particular—requires substantial efforts on the part of developers. Our goal is to keep the learner engaged in long practice sessions over many months—rather than for the short-term. In academic *research* on language learning, resources are typically scarce, and gamification usually is not considered an essential priority for allocating resources. We argue in favor of giving serious consideration to gamification in the language-learning setting—as a means of enabling in-depth research. In this paper, we introduce several gamification incentives in the Revita language-learning platform. We discuss the problems in obtaining quantitative measures of the effectiveness of gamification features.
Keywords: Language learning, Gamification, Natural language Processing, Intelligent Tutoring Systems

1. Introduction

Learning a language toward intermediate or advanced levels requires a massive investment of time on the part of the learner. Some statistics from the Foreign Service Institute, USA,[1], in Table 1, show the number of *contact* hours required for an English speaker, on average, to reach upper-intermediate level of proficiency, typically needed for diplomatic service.

In principle, a language learning platform can serve as a powerful research tool. On one hand, it can provide real value to learners. On the other hand, it can provide invaluable data to researchers—about possible learning paths, common patterns of mistakes, etc.,—which can drive research in educational data science (EDS), learning analytics, and computational didactics. We believe this kind of data is essential for real progress in EDS—we need to collect data on a massive scale, tracking learner progress over time.

This kind of longitudinal data cannot be collected without engaging the learner over extended periods of time. If the platform offers limited learning content, a "toy" learning environment, or repetitive, monotonous means of engagement, then it will allow us to collect sufficient data to serve as a foundation for in-depth research.

Gamification is the strategic attempt to enhance systems, services, and activities to create a user experience akin to playing a game—in order to engage and motivate users. Game-design elements and principles are implemented in several non-gaming contexts, including education, data collection, and data labeling (Chamberlain et al., 2013; von Ahn et al., 2006).

In this paper, we discuss several gamification strategies applied in an Intelligent Tutoring system (ITS) for language learning, Revita[2], and discuss the impacts that gamification has achieved so far in this experimental setting. Revita—a project for supporting intermediate-to-advanced language learners—is an international collaboration between several European universities. The collaborators include specialists in language teaching and didactics, currently with hundreds of university students using the platform on a regular basis. The experimental setting we describe involves applying Revita in the context of several universities.

Language	*Hours*
French, German, Italian, Portuguese, Romanian, Spanish, Swedish, Dutch, Norwegian, Afrikaans	600
Indonesian, Malaysian, Swahili	850
Albanian, Amharic, Azerbaijani, Bulgarian, Finnish, Greek, Hebrew, Hindi, Hungarian, Icelandic, Khmer, Latvian, Nepali, Polish, Russian, Serbian, Tagalog, Thai, Turkish, Urdu, Vietnamese, Zulu	1,100
Georgian, Mongolian	1,600
Arabic, Chinese, Japanese, Korean	2,200
Compare:	
4 years of college (8 semesters × 50 hr)	400
Child reaching fluency (2–4 years × 10 hr/day)	7.5–15K

Table 1: Estimates of *contact hours* required for native English speakers to reach fluency in various languages, on average. (Statistics: Foreign Service Institute)

In this paper, we evaluate the effectiveness of gamification incentives in Revita and discuss the preliminary results and problems highlighted by the evaluation. We believe that research in gamification can facilitate personalized tutoring and enhance the learning experience—which in turn will improve learner engagement, and lead to a positive feedback loop: more

[1]`www.state.gov/foreign-language-training/`

[2]`https://revita.cs.helsinki.fi`

learner data enables the development of better models, which provides a better service to the learners.
The paper is organized as follows. Section 2 reviews relevant prior work. Section 3, reviews the Revita platform for language learning toward advanced levels. Section 4 describes "hard-value"—or *competency*-related—incentives in the learning system. In Section 5, we discuss "soft-value"—or *enjoyment*-related—incentives supported or planned in system. In Section 6, we discuss a preliminary evaluation of the gamification elements in our experimental environment. In Section 7, we summarize the contributions and the future work.

2. Prior Work

2.1. GWAP

GWAP—games with a purpose, introduced in (von Ahn, 2006)—is using games to leverage human brain power to solve open problems. As a side effect of the game, annotated data is collected. von Ahn and Dabbish (2008) propose three general gaming mechanisms:

- Output agreement games: Players are randomly paired, and given a shared visible input. They attempt to achieve agreement with each other on output (not shared).
- Inversion problem games: Players are randomly paired. One plays as the describer, while the other plays as the guesser.
- Input agreement game: Two randomly paired players are given an input object. They need to describe the inputs to each other, to decide whether their inputs are the same.

Research on games and psychology shows that 8 major elements make games entertaining and enjoyable (Koster, 2004; Sweetser and Wyeth, 2005; Csikszentmihalyi, 1991):

- Concentration
- Challenge
- Immersion
- Supporting player skills
- Clear goals
- Feedback
- Social interaction
- Player's sense of being in control

These gamification principles are taken into consideration in several GWAP applications, some of which have proven to be effective for collecting data from users. For example, von Ahn et al. (2006) and Ho et al. (2009) work on image recognition. Chamberlain et al. (2013), Madge et al. (2019b), Madge et al. (2019a) and Fort et al. (2014), work on text annotation. Several papers focus on collecting data for recommendation systems (Walsh and Golbeck, 2010; Banks et al., 2015) and knowledge repositories (Herdagdelen and Baroni, 2010; Herdağdelen and Baroni, 2012) via GWAP.

2.2. ITS

Computer-assisted language learning (CALL) is a research area introduced over 50 years ago. CALL is broadly defined as "the search for and study of applications of the computer in language teaching and learning" (Levy, 1997). It is not intended to be a replacement for the teacher. As CALL developed, ITS emerged with the goal of "computer as a tutor." ITSs have been adopted in various knowledge domains, including mathematics, sciences and language learning (Slavuj et al., 2015). One popular language-learning ITS is Duolingo.[3]
A key goal of ITS is to model the learners' knowledge and skill levels. Several approaches have been proposed, including Bayesian Knowledge Tracing (BKT) (Corbett and Anderson, 1994), Learning Factor Analysis (Cen et al., 2006), and its more advanced variant, Performance Factor Analysis (Pavlik Jr et al., 2009). In this paper, we discuss the application of the Elo rating system designed for zero-sum games.

3. Language Learning Platform

Revita is a freely available online platform, for supporting language learning/tutoring *beyond the beginner level*, (Katinskaia et al., 2017; Katinskaia et al., 2018). Many free and commercial resources and applications exist on the Web, which support beginners, some with millions of users. However, once the learner has passed the beginner level, and reached low-intermediate to advanced (LI-A) level—i.e., above A1/A2 on the CEFR scale—resources available to her become drastically limited. As surveys show, very few systems today provide substantial support for LI-A learners in multiple languages.
The Revita language-learning system primarily targets "high-stakes" learners—users who are invested in the learning for the long run, and have an internal motivation for learning, such as the need to pass university courses, for work, citizenship, etc.
Revita currently supports several languages—in various stages of development, ranging from initial, "beta" versions to fairly well-developed ones. The languages include "big" languages—Finnish, Russian, Italian$^{\beta}$, German$^{\beta}$, Kazakh$^{\beta}$, Swedish$^{\beta}$, Mandarin$^{\beta}$—and several endangered minority languages, including many Finno-Ugric languages in Russia.
Revita builds on educational data collected through a collaborative effort with language teachers at several universities. In this paper, we focus on the evaluation in our experimental setting, at several major universities, where hundreds of students enroll in Russian language courses at various levels. The teachers suggest to their students to use Revita to solidify their knowledge through practice sessions, and to prepare for exams. Currently, we collect data about the students' progress in three practice contexts:

Story exercises: Students practice by doing exercises based on texts. One set of exercises is given for each

[3]https://www.duolingo.com

snippet of the text—about one paragraph. Each exercise is linked to one or more linguistic "concepts"—technically known as *constructs*. Each concept is a "skill" that the learner must master, for example: the usage of genitive plural nouns belonging to a certain paradigm, or verb government, etc. The inventory of concepts for a well-developed language is many hundreds, up to about 1.5 thousand. The user response data for each exercise contains: the correct answer, student answer (if incorrect), concepts linked to the exercise, timestamp. The system offers various types of exercises: multiple-choice questions, "cloze" (fill-in-the-blank) questions, listening comprehension, etc. These exercises are generated automatically based on the text chosen by the learner.

Flashcards: While working with texts, the students can request translations for any unfamiliar words. All requested translations are stored in the student's deck of flashcards. Students practice their vocabulary by playing with flashcards, in batches with *timed repetition*. Two types of flashcards are currently available: translation, and gender selection—important for German, French, Swedish, etc., languages where the gender of most nouns is not obvious from the noun's form. The response data consists of: student's answers to a flashcard, timestamp. Learners can upload and edit their own flashcards. We assume that the reason a learner clicked a word in text for translation is because it is unfamiliar. Also, the sentence/context where the word was encountered is attached to each flashcard as a hint.

Tests: Students can take online tests through the platform (for some of the languages). Teachers can configure the topics of the test items and their number. Items are sampled from a database of about 2000+ multiple-choice questions. The test can also be *adaptive*, where the system picks the items depending in the learner's previous questions. Tests are timed—each question has a time limit, typically 30 seconds. Like the story exercises, each test item is linked to one of the concepts implemented for the language. The questions are prepared by language teachers and linguistic experts, e.g., (Kopotev, 2012; Kopotev, 2010). At the time of this writing, the response data consists of 875000 test answers, by over 5000 learners. For each question, the system records to which concept the question belongs, whether the answer was correct, and a timestamp.

4. Improving Competency as Incentive

A crucial aspect of gamification is providing value—or incentives—to motivate users to practice longer. We can informally distinguish two kinds of value: "hard" value relates to improving competency and growing skills; "soft" value relates to spending time in an entertaining and enjoyable fashion. In the context of high-stakes language learners, the primary motivation is obtaining *hard value* from the learning system by increasing competency. However, that does not mean no other motivators are in play. In fact, we believe that "soft value" or *enjoyment incentives*—discussed in the next section—affect the user's involvement in the learning process in equal measure with hard value incentives.

We next briefly discuss what we consider to be the primary hard-value incentives that Revita offers to learners: *interesting content, assessment, and feedback*. As a learner interacts with a human teacher, she expects to receive all of these, in order to stimulate and guide her progress toward linguistic mastery. Thus it is reasonable for an automated tutoring system to aim to provide similar value.

Assessment of user performance is considered to be an important incentive. Assessment brings incentives not only on the personal level, but also on the social level—since students can compare their performance with classmates, or other learners in the platform.

4.1. User-selected Content

A key motivator in Revita's approach is encouraging the learner to select arbitrary authentic texts—which correspond with her own, personal interest *outside* the language learning context—and using this arbitrary chosen material as content for learning. This is done by automatically generating a wide variety of exercises based on the text content chosen by the user, using language technology and AI. This is a key principle in the Revita approach to tutoring.

The principle is based on the assumption that if the learner can work with topics that pose an inherent interest to her—independently of the language learning objectives—then she will spend more time engaging with the content, and hence more time practicing. Recall, our overall goal is to maximize the time which the learner invests in practicing with the language.

4.2. Elo Ratings for Language Learning

Revita adopts the Elo rating system to rate learners. The Elo rating system was originally developed for chess, and has received wide acceptance in many of the currently popular online and e-sport games. Earlier attempts have been made to apply Elo in the context of ITS, (Klinkenberg et al., 2011; Pelánek, 2016).

The Elo rating system is designed for zero-sum games, and is usually applied for Player vs. Player games (PvP). Its formula defines the **expected** result of actor A in a match against actor B according to the formula:

$$E_A = \frac{1}{1 + 10^{\frac{R_B - R_A}{\sigma}}} \tag{1}$$

E_A is the expectation (probability) that actor A will succeed, or win. R_X refers to the current Elo rating of actor X, and σ is a scaling factor.

After a match with another actor is completed, the rating of actor A is updated according to the formula:

$$R_A^{i+1} = R_A^i + K(S_A - E_A) \tag{2}$$

where S_A refers to the actual score achieved by actor A in the match: loss, draw and win for A are counted as 0,

0.5 and 1 points, respectively. The factor K determines the maximal change in the rating at one time.

In Revita, the Elo equations are used so that, rather than playing against each other, users "play against" exercises in a text, language concepts, or vocabulary items. Revita scores users in the various practice modes: story exercises, flashcards, and tests. Experiments have shown that this approach to rating the user's competency gives consistent results between the exercise Elo rating and the test Elo rating, and correlates well with external competency judgements made independently by human teachers, (Hou et al., 2019).

4.2.1. Elo Ratings in Tests

In the test setting, one "match" refers to attempt by a student to answer a question related to a given concept from the concept inventory. The two rated "actors" are the student and the concept. The rating R_A of student A represents the ability of the student. The rating R_C of a question involving concept C models the *difficulty* of the concept.

One difference compared to the original Elo system, is that students have some chance of guessing correctly on *multiple-choice* problems. To compensate for this bias, Revita adopts the approach recommended by Pelánek (2016), penalizing the expected value by the probability that a random guess is correct:

$$E_A = \frac{1}{k} \cdot 1 + (1 - \frac{1}{k}) \cdot \frac{1}{1 + 10^{\frac{R_C - R_A}{\sigma}}}, \quad (3)$$

where k is the number of choices in the multiple-choice question.

We expect that the Elo ratings for concepts will approach their "true" value after a large number of data points—"games," or test answers—have been collected from learners. To improve the quality of concept ratings, they are learned by re-adjusting all ratings by replaying all games in chronological order over several epochs. This corresponds to the Elo "*burn-in*" period, used to obtain stable ratings for all concepts currently implemented in the system for the given language.

4.2.2. Elo Ratings in Story Exercises

Revita generates exercises for each snippet of text (about one paragraph), one snippet at a time. Exercises are of different types. Each exercise is linked to one or more linguistic concept. An exercise can be rated by taking the maximum rating of the concepts linked to the exercise.

Alternatively, the system can make the simplifying assumption that the exercises in a given text will correspond *on average* to the *difficulty* of the entire text. Revita currently has models that estimate the difficulty of a text for several languages. When the learner selects a text and uploads it to the system, its difficulty is estimated by a model trained on a corpus of texts whose difficulty had been manually rated by experts.

Modeling the difficulty of a text—or its readability, complexity, etc.—is a well-studied problem, (Dubay, 2009). The model can use lexical and grammatical features, e.g., (Chen and Meurers, 2016; Heilman et al., 2008). Revita uses linear models and standard features, recommended, e.g., by Kincaid et al. (1975), Flesch (1979), and Chen and Meurers (2016), to estimate the difficulty of a text: including lexical frequency, mean token length, mean sentence length, etc.

When the exercise rating is defined in terms of average text difficulty, S_A can again denote the actual score that student A received when answering a given exercise. E_A for the exercise is assigned according to the difficulty of the text, from which the exercises are drawn.

The output of the model is scaled onto the Elo rating scale. This allows the system to estimate the performance of any rated learner on any rated text. The learner's Elo is updated after *each* answer. Further, the system updates the Elo rating of the entire text *relative to this learner* after a complete pass by the learner through the text. The rationale for updating the relative difficulty of the text is that every time the learner goes through the text, the text becomes more familiar, and therefore relatively "easier" for the given learner. Note, that since Revita selects the exercises presented to the user on each pass randomly, the actual exercises will, in general, be different on repeated passes through the text.

4.2.3. Elo Ratings in Flashcards

In the context of practicing with flashcards, the notion of a "game" is similar to the notion of a game in the context of story-based exercises, above. S_A is defined as the actual score that student A received when attempting a batch of flashcards, for example, 20 or 50. The expectation E_A for a batch of flashcards is the average Elo score of each flashcard (word). The Elo score of a flashcard/word is scaled from its Inverse Document Frequency (IDF), which is considered to be a good estimate of its difficulty level. The scaling is a mapping from the ranges of lexical frequencies to the corresponding ranges of Elo scores; this is done by experts in language pedagogy.

4.3. Feedback

In the story-based exercise mode, the learner can make *multiple attempts* to answer an exercise. After the learner answers the exercise, the system does not simply reply "correct" or "incorrect," and show the learner the correct answer in case the answer was incorrect. Rather, after each attempt, for each exercise that has not yet been answered correctly, the system returns to the learner personalized *feedback* based on her answers. Feedback comes in the form of additional hints, which *gradually* guide the learner toward the correct answer. The goal is to help the user to learn to arrive at the correct answer on her own, by developing the habit of searching the context of the exercise for clues, which indicate the correct answer.

This graduated feedback follows the foundational didactic principles of Dynamic Assessment in second

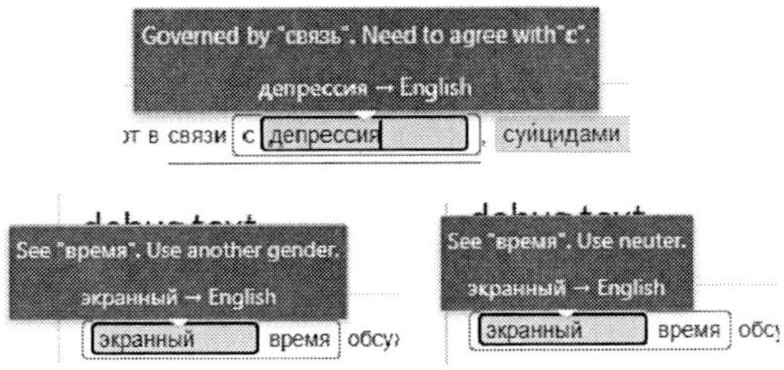

Figure 1: Examples of feedback for story exercises (in Russian). The green part of the tool-tip contains feedback to the learner: why her answer is incorrect, and hints about how to correct it. (The user can click on the blue part to request a translation for the given word, which is available for *all* words in the text).

language teaching, e.g., (Poehner, 2008). Revita's feedback module 1. analyzes the learner's answer, and 2. tries to establish which hints are most suitable, given how the learner has answered so far. Feedback is based on syntactic information found in the context of the exercise. For example, agreement—elements of a noun phrase must agree in number, case, gender, etc.—or syntactic government—a verb has certain *valence*, or its arguments are required to be in a certain case, etc.

Feedback is also based on a detailed *hierarchy* of linguistic features—which features of a word or phrase have higher priority than other features. For example, the priorities for language L might indicate that if a verb form is incorrect, then the learner should first try to get the correct mood and tense—before correcting the person and number. This hierarchy of priorities are defined in collaboration with experts in linguistics and didactics, for each language.

Figure 1 shows examples of feedback that a learner may receive after attempting to answer a story exercise. The circled border shows the phrase structure surrounding the cloze exercise, and hints at the *agreement* relationships that must not be violated within the phrase. The blue underline shows that there is a *government* relationship between the verb and a phrase that it governs. The green part of the tool-tip contains the feedback and hints that the user receives after the previous attempt.

The examples on the bottom show how the progressive feedback becomes more specific as the learner proceeds, until she finds the correct answer—or exceeds the maximum number of attempts. On the left, the hint says that the gender is incorrect; on the right, it gives the specific gender needed in this context.

5. Enjoyment as Incentive

As discussed in (von Ahn and Dabbish, 2008)—in the context of GWAP—users play not (only) because they are personally interested in solving an instance of a computational problem, but because they like to be entertained.

We next describe several features that Revita tries to provide as enjoyment incentives.

5.1. Crossword

The crossword stimulates further practicing with grammar and vocabulary problems based on the text that the user may have worked with earlier, but while working in a different setting, which is more akin to solving a puzzle. A crossword is based on any text chosen by the learner; words in the crossword are automatically and randomly selected from the text. To complete the crossword, the learner inserts each missing word into the story, in its correct inflected form. The clues are the translations of the missing words, rather than their lemmas, as in story-based exercises. Figure 2 shows an example of a crossword built from a news story.

5.2. Social Interaction

Friend and Sharing: As a social feature in Revita, it allows learners to share any content that they find interesting. Stories can be shared among friends, with a message attached. When a learner shares a story with another, an email notification is sent. The receiver can accept or reject the shared content, and accept the sender as a "friend", so future sharing will require no notification, or block the sender. User can also share arbitrary own *notes* that they can attach anywhere in the story.

Sharing with a group of learners is also possible. A teacher can create a group, and invite learners into the group. This feature supports the collaboration with teachers, since it allows the teacher to supervise a class of students. The teacher can invite them to join a group through the platform (which requires an email confirmation by the student), or send the invitees an encrypted pass-key to the group.

Competition Mode: The competition mode in Revita is related to story-based exercises. Regular exercises, described in section 4.2.2, allow the user unlimited time to answer. The purpose of the competition mode is to challenge the learners to make correct answers, but under time constraints.

In competition mode, the learner and the opponent work on identical exercises (based on the story chosen by the learner). The objective is to complete the exercises faster than the opponent, while making fewer mistakes than the opponent. The competition ends when one of the players—the learner or the opponent—reaches the end of the story. Whoever answered more exercises correctly is the winner. This effectively combines the drive for A. answering exercises correctly, and B. doing so within shorter time.

Revita creates an opponent—a "bot"—with which the learner will compete. The bot's parameters are tuned to match the human learner's previous performance: the learner's own reading speed, the learner's answering speed, and the learner's answer accuracy—these are all calculated based on the learner's past history.

Figure 2: Example of crossword for a story (in Finnish). Left to right: the crossword board, the text, the clue and translation box.

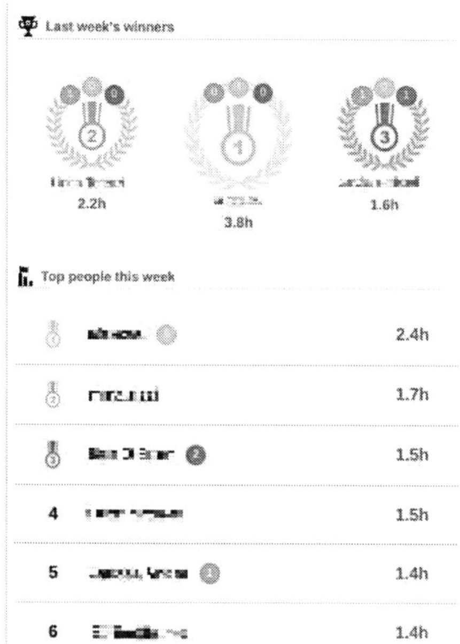

Figure 3: Leaderboard for *time spent* practicing on the platform. The board shows the top 3 learners from last week, and the leaders for the running week. Previous leaderboard achievements are denoted by numbers inside gold, silver and bronze medals. (The users' names have been blurred to protect their privacy.)

Thus, the bot aims to imitate a learner's performance as closely as possible. In this way, the learner is assured that the opponent is optimally matched to her skills—not much weaker and not much stronger. Since the opponent is optimally matched to the learner, the competition is optimally challenging, and the learner is essentially trying to surpass *her own prior performance*—to reach above her current skill level.

In the future, we plan to collect more detailed information about the learner's performance, e.g.: key-stroke frequency, expected response time per concept, etc.

Leaderboards and Achievements: Learners pass milestones on several metrics; currently the system awards "achievements" to the user based on A. the amount of time spent practicing, B. the number of stories the learner has uploaded to the system, and C. the number of stories the learner has practiced through to completion. Each of these metrics has five milestones. Once the learner reaches a milestone, a permanent badge will appear in the learner's achievement collection.

In addition, to encourage a wider-scale competition, Revita maintains a weekly *leaderboard*, tracking the time that the learners spend practicing across all types of exercises.[4] The three top performers each week also receive an achievement—a medal. Figure 3 shows a example leaderboard from a recent week.

6. Evaluation

Our experimental setting involves analyzing data from students at several European universities who are studying Russian and using Revita in conjunction with their coursework. The experimental period spans 10 months—41 weeks—from beginning of July 2021 through beginning of April 2022 (the time of this publication). We chose to begin compiling statistics in July, because that was the time when several major improvements to the support for Russian were released, which spurred the language teachers toward heavier utilization of the system in their teaching.

The activity of the students is recorded in Revita's database. At the time of this writing, the learning activities for which timing information is available in Revita include: story-based exercises, flashcard exercises, creation of new flashcards (which means that the user requested a translation for some unfamiliar word, thereby adding new flashcards to her card deck), and reading a story (without doing exercises).

Other activities—crosswords, competitions, etc.—at present do not have timing information recorded in the database. Therefore, these activities are not included in the present study; they will be the subject of more in-depth investigations on the impacts of gamification on learning in the near future.

[4]To ensure privacy, learners will appear in the leaderboard only if they agree to show their record.

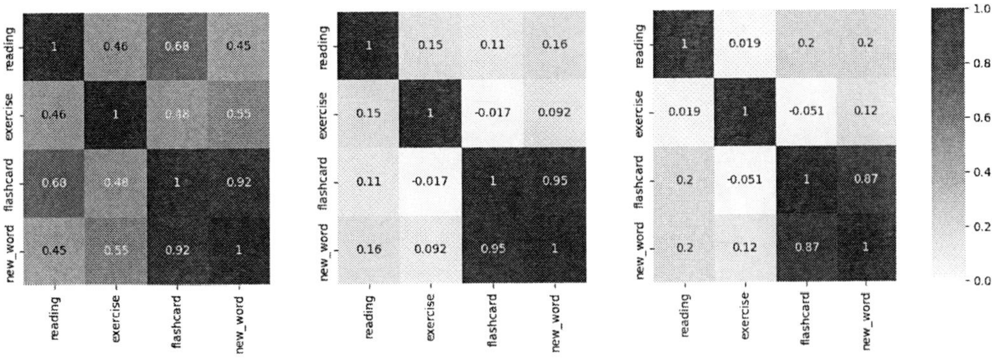

Figure 4: Correlation matrix between four types of user activities, for three populations: top 200 most active students (left), 200–400 (middle), and 400–600 (right).

6.1. Correlation between activities

The matrices in Figure 4 show the pairwise correlations between the various learning activities, for several "populations" of students. We examine the 600 most active students during this period, and split them into three groups according to their activity rank: 0–200, 200–400, and 400–600. Activities labeled *flashcard*, story *exercise* and *new word* indicate the total number of items that a user has answered while practicing with flashcards and story exercises, and the number of translation lookups for unfamiliar words, respectively. We can make several observations from the Figure. The matrices show a high correlation between the *flashcards* and the *new word*.

This is very encouraging, since it shows that those learners who frequently request translations for unfamiliar words, also come back at a later time to practice with the vocabulary flashcards that they have collected over time—rather than looking up translations and never taking the trouble to review them and practice with them.

The lighter squares in the correlation matrix for the top-200 students also provide an interesting insight: they indicate a lower correlation between reading and the creation of new cards (*new word*). That means that people tend to look up unfamiliar words more during exercising than during reading. At the same time, the correlation between reading and card-based exercise is higher than the correlation between reading and story-based exercise. This may suggest that some people prefer to practice with the vocabulary flashcards after reading a story. This confirms that there is *added value* in offering multiple kinds of activities in the system, since different people prefer different activities.

Lastly, we can see that when we move from the top-200 population to the others, all correlations drop substantially (except the correlation between flashcard practice and new words, mentioned above). This may mean that the activities in which the "less-motivated" students engage are less varied and less spread out, more concentrated on one (or very few) types of activities. These observations are further explored in Section 6.4.

6.2. Weekly time spent on practice

The learners in our experimental setting are mainly university students: they are high-stakes users, since working with Revita is part of their curricular activity. The metrics presented in this section show the amount of activity during the given time period.

We measure the time that the students invest in working with Revita. Figure 5 shows the total activity time of the top 200 most active learners across the 41-week experimental period. The patterns that emerge from the Figure reflect the real-world situation:

- Reduced activity between semesters, and at the start of a new semester when students are being introduced to system: Dec 2021–Feb 2022,
- More activity in the middle of semester: Oct 2021–Nov 2021, and Feb 2022–Apr 2022,
- A spike of activity toward the end of semester and near exams: Aug 2021–Sept 2021.

6.3. Correlation between practice and leaderboards

Since the students invested considerably more time from September 2021, during these weeks we calculated the correlation between the user's *leaderboard position* (rank) on a given week N, and extra time spent on during the *following* week $N+1$ compared to week N. The correlations were computed only for students who reached a top-10 position during any of the 41 weeks of activity. The result is a positive correlation of 0.50, which suggests that a high rank on the leaderboard tends to measurably stimulate also more activity during the following week!

This suggests that being closer to the top is a strong motivator for students to work harder: that the leaderboard is an effective incentive to motivate our learners. The leaderboard may have a limited influence on students who do not achieve a relatively high rank. The leaderboard currently indicates only the student's absolute rank, rather than a relative position. We plan to

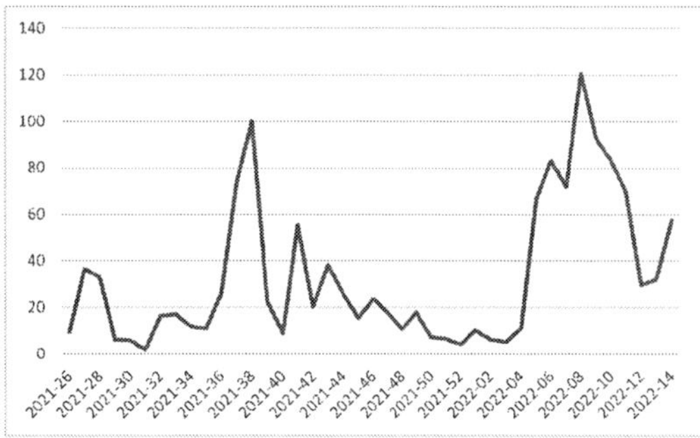

Figure 5: Total weekly hours spent, for 600 most active learners over the last 10 months.

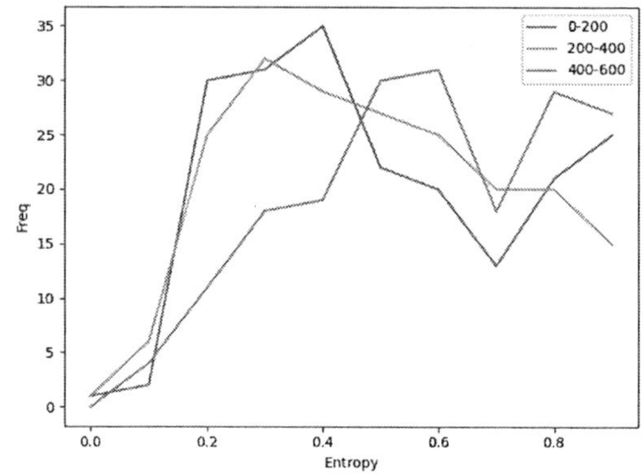

Figure 6: Histogram: entropy of activity of 600 most active users, for 3 populations: top 200 most active students (blue), 200–400 (orange), 400–600 (green). Y-axis: count of students with given entropy.

show also the *relative* percentage in the leaderboard, and check how that will influence all users: are they incentivized to move toward the top if they are told they are in the top 10%? top 20% ? top 50%?

6.4. Learner engagement across activities

For the 600 most active learners during the experimental period, we compute another indicator: the *entropy* of the distribution of the user's time across *different* activity types—namely: story exercises, flashcards, and flashcard creation by looking up new words.[5] We compute the entropy based on the distribution of time across these three classes of activity.[6] This distribution models the "probability" that the user will engage in activity i as simply $\frac{t_i}{\sum_j t_j}$, where $t(i)$ is the amount of time she spent on activity $i \in \{\text{exercise, flashcard, new word}\}$.

One possible conjecture would be that users who spend *more* time on the platform engage in—therefore, *prefer*—a more varied set of activities; that "breaking the monotony" helps the most active users keep the motivation to practice on the platform longer.

Figure 6 is a visualization of the histograms of entropies for the most active 600 users, sub-divided into 3 populations. We make some observations based on these activity entropies across the users. Recall, that the entropies are computed over three kinds of activities (at present). For the top-200 students (blue), the entropy is mostly concentrated on the left side of the graph, for students ranked 200–400 (orange), the entropy moves to the right, and for the least active it's concentrated most on the right. This suggests that the less dedicated learners—who spend less time—tend to "scatter" their time more on different activities. The "bimodal" histogram of the top-200 suggests that these users study with different styles: most focus on few activities (low entropy), while some engage in a variety of activities, spending their time more uniformly.

This also supports the conjecture in Section 6.1: that the most engaged users don't simply click around on words just to get a translation in the moment, when they encounter unfamiliar vocabulary; they actually come back to practice with their flashcards at a later time.

7. Conclusions

In this paper we discuss the range of activities and gamification features that are available at present to users of the Revita ITS. The main contribution is the presentation of our efforts to measure the impacts of the activities and gamification on the effectiveness of learning. Our experiments track a population of 600 learners using Revita at several universities. A key goal in ITS is to provide students with *personalized* learning and support their individual learning process. Achieving this goal requires strong learner engagement.

We explore how offering a variety of activities and gamification—rather than only a narrow selection of exercise types—may help learning, by keeping the learners more engaged. Most importantly, obtaining solid quantitative proof of these conjectures is not a trivial task, and requires extensive longitudinal studies with large numbers of users. Such studies require systems that are sufficiently friendly so that users would be willing to use them for many months at a time. Without actual such systems, conducting in-depth research on engagement is not possible.

In Revita, the gamification efforts are in the early stages, and currently not guided by specific theoretical or precedent-based justifications. We believe that the data we gather from these efforts will help establish new precedents and theoretical foundations.

Future work will include expanding the gamification features of Revita, and more thorough evaluations of learner engagement. We plan to track a more extensive inventory of user activities, which we hope will lead to further interesting findings.

[5] Story *reading* is not included in this calculation, because it is not directly comparable with other activities for now.

[6] Entropy in Figure 6 is normalized to be in $[0, 1]$ by using $\log_3$, since we have 3 classes—the three types of activity.

Acknowledgements

This work was supported in part by the Academy of Finland, Helsinki Institute for Information Technology (HIIT), BusinessFinland (Grant "Revita", 42560/31/2020), and Future Development Fund, Faculty of Arts, University of Helsinki.

8. Bibliographical References

Banks, S., Rafter, R., and Smyth, B. (2015). The recommendation game: Using a game-with-a-purpose to generate recommendation data. In *Proceedings of the 9th ACM Conference on Recommender Systems*, pages 305–308.

Cen, H., Koedinger, K., and Junker, B. (2006). Learning factors analysis – a general method for cognitive model evaluation and improvement. In Mitsuru Ikeda, et al., editors, *Intelligent Tutoring Systems*, pages 164–175, Berlin, Heidelberg. Springer Berlin Heidelberg.

Chamberlain, J., Fort, K., Kruschwitz, U., Lafourcade, M., and Poesio, M. (2013). Using Games to Create Language Resources: Successes and Limitations of the Approach. In Gurevych, et al., editors, *Theory and Applications of Natural Language Processing*, page 42. Springer, January.

Chen, X. and Meurers, D. (2016). Characterizing text difficulty with word frequencies. In *Proceedings of the 11th Workshop on Innovative Use of NLP for Building Educational Applications*, pages 84–94.

Corbett, A. T. and Anderson, J. R. (1994). Knowledge tracing: Modeling the acquisition of procedural knowledge. *User modeling and user-adapted interaction*, 4(4):253–278.

Csikszentmihalyi, M. (1991). *Flow: The Psychology of Optimal Experience*. Harper Perennial, New York, NY, March.

Dubay, W. (2009). Unlocking Language: The classic readability studies. *Professional Communication, IEEE Transactions on*, 51:416 – 417, 01.

Flesch, R. (1979). How to write plain English: Let's start with the formula. *University of Canterbury*.

Fort, K., Guillaume, B., and Chastant, H. (2014). Creating zombilingo, a game with a purpose for dependency syntax annotation. In *Proceedings of the First International Workshop on Gamification for Information Retrieval*, pages 2–6.

Heilman, M., Collins-Thompson, K., and Eskenazi, M. (2008). An analysis of statistical models and features for reading difficulty prediction. In *Proceedings of the third workshop on innovative use of NLP for building educational applications*, pages 71–79. Association for Computational Linguistics.

Herdagdelen, A. and Baroni, M. (2010). The concept game: Better commonsense knowledge extraction by combining text mining and a game with a purpose. In *2010 AAAI Fall Symposium Series*.

Herdağdelen, A. and Baroni, M. (2012). Bootstrapping a game with a purpose for commonsense collection. *ACM Transactions on Intelligent Systems and Technology (TIST)*, 3(4):1–24.

Ho, C.-J., Chang, T.-H., Lee, J.-C., Hsu, J. Y.-j., and Chen, K.-T. (2009). KissKissBan: A competitive human computation game for image annotation. In *Proceedings of the ACM SIGKDD Workshop on Human Computation*, pages 11–14.

Hou, J., Koppatz, M. W., Quecedo, J. M. H., Stoyanova, N., Kopotev, M., and Yangarber, R. (2019). Modeling language learning using specialized Elo ratings. In *Proceedings of the 14th Workshop on Innovative Use of NLP for Building Educational Applications, ACL: 56th annual meeting of the Association for Computational Linguistics*.

Katinskaia, A., Nouri, J., and Yangarber, R. (2017). Revita: a system for language learning and supporting endangered languages. In *6th Workshop on NLP for CALL and 2nd Workshop on NLP for Research on Language Acquisition, at NoDaLiDa*, Gothenburg, Sweden.

Katinskaia, A., Nouri, J., and Yangarber, R. (2018). Revita: a language-learning platform at the intersection of ITS and CALL. In *Proceedings of LREC: 11th International Conference on Language Resources and Evaluation*, Miyazaki, Japan.

Kincaid, J. P., Fishburne Jr, R. P., Rogers, R. L., and Chissom, B. S. (1975). Derivation of new readability formulas (automated readability index, fog count and Flesch reading ease formula) for Navy enlisted personnel.

Klinkenberg, S., Straatemeier, M., and van der Maas, H. L. (2011). Computer adaptive practice of maths ability using a new item response model for on-the-fly ability and difficulty estimation. *Computers & Education*, 57(2):1813–1824.

Kopotev, M. (2010). Система прогрессивного тестирования Karttu: описание и первые результаты (The Karttu system for progressive testing: description and initial results). Русский язык за рубежом *(Russian language abroad)*, (3):23–29.

Kopotev, M. (2012). Karttu: результаты языкового тестирования в школе и вузе (Karttu: results of language testing in schools and universities). Формирование и оценка коммуникативной компетенции билингвов в процессе двуязычного образования (Formation and assessment of communicative competency of bilinguals in bilingual education), pages 312–339.

Koster, R. (2004). *A Theory of Fun for Game Design*. Paraglyph Press.

Levy, M. (1997). *Computer-assisted language learning: Context and conceptualization*. Oxford University Press.

Madge, C., Bartle, R., Chamberlain, J., Kruschwitz, U., and Poesio, M. (2019a). Making text annotation fun with a clicker game. In *Proceedings of the 14th In-*

ternational Conference on the Foundations of Digital Games*, New York, NY, USA. Association for Computing Machinery.

Madge, C., Bartle, R., Chamberlain, J., Kruschwitz, U., and Poesio, M. (2019b). Incremental game mechanics applied to text annotation. In *Proceedings of the Annual Symposium on Computer-Human Interaction in Play*, pages 545–558.

Pavlik Jr, P. I., Cen, H., and Koedinger, K. R. (2009). Performance factors analysis–a new alternative to knowledge tracing. *Online Submission*.

Pelánek, R. (2016). Applications of the Elo rating system in adaptive educational systems. *Computers & Education*, 98:169–179.

Poehner, M. E. (2008). *Dynamic assessment: A Vygotskian approach to understanding and promoting L2 development*, volume 9. Springer Science & Business Media.

Slavuj, V., Kovačić, B., and Jugo, I. (2015). Intelligent tutoring systems for language learning. In *Proceedings of the 38th International Convention on Information and Communication Technology, Electronics and Microelectronics (MIPRO)*. IEEE.

Sweetser, P. and Wyeth, P. (2005). GameFlow: A model for evaluating player enjoyment in games. *Computers in Entertainment*, 3(3):3, July.

von Ahn, L. and Dabbish, L. (2008). Designing games with a purpose. *Communications of the ACM*, 51(8):58–67, August.

von Ahn, L., Liu, R., and Blum, M. (2006). Peekaboom: A game for locating objects in images. In *Proceedings of the SIGCHI Conference on Human Factors in Computing Systems*, page 55–64, New York, NY, USA. Association for Computing Machinery.

von Ahn, L. (2006). Games with a purpose. *Computer*, 39(6):92–94.

Walsh, G. and Golbeck, J. (2010). Curator: a game with a purpose for collection recommendation. In *Proceedings of the SIGCHI Conference on Human Factors in Computing Systems*, pages 2079–2082.

Proceedings of the 9th Games and Natural Language Processing Workshop @LREC2022, pages 17–27
Marseille, 25 June 2022

Less Text, More Visuals: Evaluating The Onboarding Phase in a GWAP for NLP

Fatima Althani, Chris Madge, Massimo Poesio
Queen Mary Univ. Of London, United Kingdom
{f.althani, c.j.madge, m.poesio}@qmul.ac.uk

Abstract

Games-with-a-purpose find attracting players a challenge. To improve player recruitment, we explored two game design elements that can increase player engagement during the onboarding phase; a narrative and a tutorial. In a qualitative study with 12 players of linguistic and language learning games, we examined the effect of presentation format on players' engagement. Our reflexive thematic analysis found that in the onboarding phase of a GWAP for NLP, presenting players with visuals is expected and presenting too much text overwhelms them. Furthermore, players found that the instructions they were presented with lacked linguistic context. Additionally, the tutorial and game interface required refinement as the feedback is unsupportive and the graphics were not clear.

Keywords: Games-with-a-Purpose, Onboarding phase, Modality effect, Narratives, Tutorials

1. Introduction

Games-with-a-Purpose (GWAPs) can be a useful tool for collecting linguistic data (Poesio et al., 2013; Lafourcade, 2007; Guillaume et al., 2016). However, recruiting and retaining players of GWAPs can be a challenge. This challenge is relevant for GWAPs for NLP, as engagement is low compared to GWAPs of other domains (Von Ahn and Dabbish, 2004). One of the ways GWAPs attract players is by incorporating well-established game design elements (Segundo Díaz et al., 2022). Game design elements can enhance usability and enjoyment, which are both design strategies used to promote engagement (Doherty and Doherty, 2018). For instance, when certain game design elements are present in GWAPs, they can lead to a player's enjoyment (Segundo Díaz et al., 2022) and learnability (Andersen et al., 2012; Miller et al., 2019).

We are interested in examining enjoyment in GWAPs because enjoyment was identified as a motivator in GWAPs (Mekler et al., 2014) and can lead to player engagement (Boyle et al., 2016). Another factor that can lead to engagement in GWAPs is usability (Bowser et al., 2013; Bui et al., 2020). The usability of a game determines its success in engaging players (Hamari and Keronen, 2017). In GWAPs, learnability is a common usability issue that affects the recruitment and retention of new players. This is due to the steep learning curve found in some GWAPs that can negatively impact player engagement (Miller and Cooper, 2022).

In this study, we chose to focus on two game design elements found in a game's initial stages: the narrative and tutorial. We focused on exploring the elements related to the onboarding phase of the game, as onboarding is one of the first stages of a player's journey. At this stage, players are given a reason to play the game (Chou, 2019), and it is one of the most important stages when it comes to engaging players (Cheung et al., 2014). Engaging players of GWAPs during this stage is a significant obstacle to overcome, as player engagement at this stage is what determines long-term engagement in a game (Shelley, 2001). This indicates that designing an appealing onboarding stage in a GWAP is crucial for promoting player engagement.

While the presence of tutorials (Andersen et al., 2012) and narratives (Prestopnik and Tang, 2015; Wang et al., 2015) were previously examined in GWAPs, the role of the presentation format of those two game design elements were not evaluated. Based on Cognitive Load Theory (Kirschner, 2002), information presentation is an essential aspect of instructional design in HCI. For instance, Mayer and Moreno (2002) propose that it is better to present instructions in both visuals and text rather than text alone. Hence, we believe that understanding the impact of the presentation format is a necessary aspect to explore in GWAPs.

This study asks the following research question "How do you introduce players to a GWAP for NLP, and do the different presentation formats of the onboarding phase influence player experience?". To further explore this topic, we developed two different ways of presenting the onboarding phase of a GWAP: a (1) Text version and an (2) Animated version. Using a qualitative approach, we explore which of the two versions is more engaging. The primary contribution of this paper is providing initial design insight on what promotes player engagement in the onboarding phase of a GWAP and how different presentation formats influence their experience. Our conclusion was drawn from a reflexive thematic analysis based on several theories and frameworks, including instructional design theories (van der Meij, 1995), usability heuristics (Nielsen, 1994), and learning models (Jennett et al., 2016).

2. Related Work

2.1. Games-with-a-Purpose for NLP

Gamifying a GWAP for language labelling is challenging. Unlike GWAPs, where the player is labelling images, it is apparent that a player is labelling text, making the task less engaging (Lafourcade et al., 2015). In order to engage players, different approaches have been taken to gamify GWAPs in this domain (Lafourcade, 2007; Poesio et al., 2013; Fort et al., 2014). For instance, Phrase Detectives (Poesio et al., 2013) adopted gamification techniques to motivate players to annotate anaphoric data. Another recent example of a GWAP that implemented a gamification approach is Wormingo (Kicikoglu et al., 2019) which incorporated linguistic puzzles to engage players. In an attempt to produce a more game-like experience, TileAttack (Madge et al., 2017) applies a similar design to The ESP Game (Von Ahn and Dabbish, 2004) but for the aim of labelling text instead of images. Another game that experimented with game-like mechanics is WordClicker (Madge et al., 2019). WordClicker is a clicker game designed to collect text annotations through incremental game mechanics. To create a more engaging GWAP for NLP, LingoTowns[1] was developed, a platform that hosts several mini-games based on TileAttack, WordClicker and Wormingo. This gaming platform is represented as a virtual world and incorporates different design elements to increase player engagement. Findings (Raddick et al., 2009) suggest that GWAP players are interested in both the entertainment and educational aspect of a GWAP. Therefore, LingoTowns aim to provide a fun gaming experience while encouraging players to learn about language.

2.2. Player Engagement

Many studies have previously looked at engagement in GWAPs (Tinati et al., 2017; Bowser et al., 2013; Curtis, 2015; Greenhill et al., 2016; Iacovides et al., 2013). To further understand the role of engagement in GWAPs, we must first understand how engagement is experienced. Engagement is dynamic and multifaceted as it can be emotional, cognitive or behavioural (Zyngier, 2008; Bouta and Retalis, 2013; Islas Sedano et al., 2013). For example, in a GWAP, engagement can be experienced by either increasing a player's enjoyment (Boyle et al., 2016; Segundo Díaz et al., 2022) or by increasing a player's learnability (Andersen et al., 2012; Miller et al., 2019; Miller and Cooper, 2022). Our study mainly focuses on the emotional and cognitive aspects of engagement.

2.3. Game Design Elements

Game design elements (GDEs) allow GWAPs to become more game-like and therefore engaging. For instance, GDEs provide a game with features that can both enhance a player's enjoyment and learnability. Understanding which elements provide players with a better player experience is necessary to design successful GWAPs. Game design models and frameworks have been previously developed to examine the role of GDEs in games. A popular model is the Mechanics Design Aesthetics framework (Hunicke et al., 2004), which mainly focuses on gameplay and game mechanics. Nevertheless, Zubek (2020) highlights that many other factors apart from gameplay can influence player experience, such as the visual design of the game. For instance, a recent study (Segundo Díaz et al., 2022) has examined how to design enjoyable and engaging GWAPs by incorporating different game design elements. Several elements backed by Flow Theory (Csikszentmihalyi, 1990) were found to increase enjoyment. For instance, both narrative and tutorial were found to contribute to the player's enjoyment positively and, therefore, were examined. Novak (2015) suggests further exploring the instructional benefits of incorporating a narrative. Additionally, we are focusing on those two elements as they can be used to improve the onboarding phase.

2.4. Modality Effect

The modality in which the GDEs can be presented can influence player engagement. For instance, animations can be used to entertain players and aid in learning (Mayer and Moreno, 2002). Some studies (Palmiter et al., 1991) suggest knowledge retention is improved in text-only tutorials. Nonetheless, animations were found to help users learn faster (Palmiter and Elkerton, 1993). Modality effect was previously explored in GWAPs (de Leon Pereira et al., 2021; Mildner et al., 2015); however, the studies did not explore the presentation modes of the onboarding phase of a GWAP. Comparing two different presentation formats will help us understand what kind of effect modality has on players of GWAPs during the onboarding phase.

3. Method

3.1. Design

Participants were randomly assigned one of the two conditions; the animated or text version of the onboarding phase. We selected a between-subject study design to avoid the effects of players familiar with one interface over the other, increasing their learning effects.

3.2. LingoTowns

The game used to perform this study is LingoTowns, a new linguistic GWAP developed by our research group. LingoTowns is a procedurally generated isometric world where each town represents a unique document that needs to be annotated. The gaming platform hosts three mini-games; PhraseFarm, which is an updated version of TileAttack (Madge et al., 2017), Lingotoruim, which is an updated Wormingo (Kicikoglu et al., 2019) and CafeClicker, previously known as WordClicker (Madge et al., 2019). Each

[1] http://lingotowns.com

of the mini-games is represented by a building found within each town. For instance, the farm represents PhraseFarm, the bakery represents CafeClicker, and the library represents Lingatorium. The three mini-games allow players to annotate parts of speech. The game features a narrative where players are introduced to the context of the game. Initially, the game's presentation of the onboarding phase was designed to be text-based; however, we believe that presenting both the narrative and tutorial as an animation would increase engagement. This led us to design both a text-based version and an animated version of the onboarding phase of LingoTowns.

Description of the Onboarding Phase. The text-based version was inspired by the initial prototype of the Lingotowns' onboarding phase, which focused on introducing the story by text. To examine the effect of modality on both the narrative and tutorial, we designed an animated version of the onboarding.

Figure 1: The animated version of the narrative

The design of the animated version of the onboarding (see Figure 1 and 2) follows Mayer and Moreno (2002) multimedia learning principles. Based on the multiple representation principle, it is best to present animation along with text or audio. Therefore the presentation of the animation is provided with the text. The text is displayed on the bottom of the screen, staying close to the animation, supporting the spatial contiguity principle. The animation follows the initial narrative; however, it was edited to be more dialogue-driven to support the personalisation principle. This principle suggests presenting the text in a conversational style.

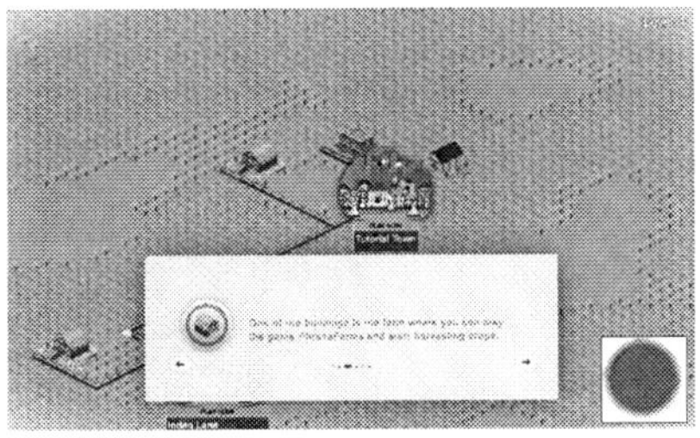

Figure 2: The animated version of the tutorial

The tutorial provided players with simple instructions on the interface to avoid cognitive load, as Hawlitschek and Joeckel (2017) found that detailed instructions in an educational game added extraneous load to the player, decreasing their learning. Hence, we did not include instructions regarding the linguistic aspect of the game in the onboarding phase. Instead, players learn more about linguistic concepts when they start playing the mini-games.

3.3. Participants

A total of 12 (Female= 9, Male= 3) participants were recruited. The mean age of the participants was approximately 30.23, with a standard deviation of 25.62. Participants were recruited from a screener survey of those interested in linguistic and language learning games using a convenience sampling approach.Participants who were interested in taking part in further research were emailed an invitation to the study. This includes 1) Participants who play language games. 2) People who reported that they would be interested in playing a linguistic or language learning game to further scientific knowledge. All participants were fully debriefed after the interview session and received a £30 gift voucher.

3.4. Procedure

In order to identify issues with the design of the experiment, a pilot was performed prior to the study. Following some usability and design fixes, a semi-structured interview was conducted. This was done to explore the users' insights into the presentation design of the onboarding phase in the game. The interviews were conducted from February 22 to March 12 with each interview lasting approximately 15 minutes. Before the study, participants were shown an informed consent where the study and research objectives were stated. The interviews were both screen and audio recorded for further analysis. Once participants were thoroughly introduced to the study, they were then given a link to access one version of the game and asked to complete the tasks. The tasks did not instruct the player to play any of the mini-games to limit any confounding variables as we only focused on LingoTowns onboarding phase and not gameplay. Participants were encouraged to be vocal about their thoughts following a think-aloud protocol (Lewis, 1982). The researcher asked participants follow-up questions after any insight, and participants were encouraged to elaborate. During the interviews, participants were asked about their experience when introduced to LingoTowns. For instance, participants were asked the following questions: *"What did you think of the onboarding phase?"* or *"How did you find the tutorial?"*. Once all tasks were completed, the researcher asked the participants for final feedback on the game.

4. Analysis

In total 182 (M= 15, SD= 3.47) minutes of data was collected[2]. Data was first transcribed and then organised by codes into an affinity diagram where themes were generated. The first author performed this analysis to explore the research question, "How do you introduce players to a GWAP and do the different presentation formats of the onboarding phase influence player experience?". This method was used due to (1) The small sample size of this study due to the niche area of interest and (2) Player experience can be greatly subjective; therefore, examining player experience more closely and understanding a player's thoughts is more valuable during this early stage. A Reflexive Thematic Analysis (Braun and Clarke, 2021) was the most appropriate analysis method for the aims of this study due to the small sample size present and its flexibility regarding theoretical approaches. Our analysis was theoretically based on instructional design theories (Van Merriënboer and Kirschner, 2017; Huang and Johnson, 2009), heuristics (Nielsen, 1994; van der Meij, 1995) and learning models (Jennett et al., 2016). We acknowledge that our position may have caused unavoidable bias when collecting and analysing data. However, throughout the data collection, participants were encouraged and reminded to voice their honest opinion and be critical of the interface they were presented with.

5. Results

5.1. Less Text, More Visuals

Presenting information entirely by text seems to be unexpected in a game, even to players of linguistic and language learning games. Players expect to be presented with visuals, whether it be an animation, video or graphics. Furthermore, too much text can overwhelm players, which increases the chances of them skipping through the tutorial. Moreover, the combination of both text and visuals in the onboarding phase can increase player engagement. Additionally, audio was expected when players were presented with the animated version of the onboarding. Nevertheless, players who were presented with text did not suggest audio. This is possibly due to them expecting audio to be present when they are viewing an animation or video.

5.1.1. Representing Narratives with Visuals is Expected

Players presented with the narrative as an animation reacted positively to it. However, they were expecting to be presented with visuals to support the narrative. Games typically engage users by introducing a game with animations or graphics. Likewise, players presented with the text version of the narrative suggested presenting the narrative with visuals. Players who were presented with the animated version found the presentation of the narrative visually appealing. As one player (P5, Animation) commented, *"I thought it looked really good. It looks really professional."* Moreover, animations are seen as a 'standard' way to introduce games:

"I thought [the animation] was kind of cute, which is probably the best way to put it the little people popping up in the little boxes. Also, it's a very standard way to introduce a game. It looked like [...] a lot of other games, like kind of the pop-ups and stuff. So it was a familiar thing to see. It didn't surprise me, but I liked it. "(P5, Animation)

While players were satisfied with the animation, they were unsure whether there was sound playing. A participant asked, *"Is there actually a sound [playing] in the background?"* (P3, Animation), And another one (P8, Animation) replied when asked why sound was expected. *"I thought they were moving their mouths. I wasn't sure if I was supposed to hear somebody.* "P8 then suggested that *"[adding] sound would make it a better experience "*. This could be due to players expecting sound from animations in general, as they are frequently present in games when an animation is playing. Adding audio could motivate players and lead to higher immersion. Game design researchers, Malone and Lepper (1987), found that sensory stimulation is a motivational technique that can be used to increase engagement. Solving this issue could increase the player's sense of flow because their attention would be focused on the animation. Meanwhile, players who were presented with the text version enjoyed the story's context but found that visuals were missing. One participant (P4, Text) commented on the narrative *"I like the fact that you came up with a story to motivate people to participate and play the games. I like it."* Another player found the story and context of the game interesting but felt like it was missing animations:

"I love the setting of it [...] Especially since the whole language has been lost, an entirely new era, it just makes me want to explore it. Now when I think of this, or start to think of little animations, where it might have the future, what it might look like and stuff like that." (P1, Text)

Having a narrative and context benefits a GWAP and makes it more meaningful to play. Another participant found the context of the story enjoyable; however, the textual presentation could be improved:

"I like the idea of the story. I just think it needs a bit more. And it could even be like a little video intro. You know, kind of take it a step further than pictures. It could be a little story with little people showing you what you need to do well in the game [...] It Doesn't need to be long. It could literally be, like, 30 seconds or something. But just enough to kind of set the scene, I suppose [...] it's good to have a story at the begin-

[2]Please contact the first author for access to full transcripts.

ning. But then you could use the same kind of theme to do the instructions as well, and that would tie it all in quite nicely together. So if you had maybe the same characters or even just things like the same font, that type of thing, [...], then that would be a good way to bring it all together." (P10, Text)

While the context of the narrative is seen as enjoyable, the presentation seems to be lacking visuals. Audio and visual effects can evoke sensory curiosity to heighten the sense of fantasy. This heuristic was proposed by Malone (1982) from a set of guidelines aimed at producing enjoyable user interfaces. Additionally, P10 (Text) recommended using visuals for the tutorial screens and the narrative. This reinforces the findings of Mayer and Moreno (2002), which suggest that multimedia presenting both texts with visuals can promote learning. Additionally, having text presented with visuals seems favourable among other players. As one participant (P1, Text) put it, *"having the text and some animations that would go with [it], would be really really engaging."* While players are expected to see visuals in the onboarding phase, they might still give the game a try without any visuals being present during the onboarding. One participant expressed that animations may not be essential, and the purpose of this game is the primary motivator to play:

"The animation seems good enough, but since it's a language game, [...] we're more focused on that aspect and not going to be looking for [good] animation". (P8, Animation)

Many players introduced to the text version would still give the game a try despite the onboarding lacking visuals:

"Would I be interested in playing a game like this? Probably, yes. Not because of how it looks; it would be nearly just what it's about, like reading about that. It's about lingo, and language is something that interests me. So would I be interested in a game like this? Absolutely. Would I see this game randomly without maybe knowing what it's about and be interested? Probably not." (P7, Animation)

This perspective is supported by previous studies (Raddick et al., 2009; Causer, 2012; Crowston and Prestopnik, 2013; Iacovides et al., 2013; Curtis, 2015; Eveleigh et al., 2014; Jennett et al., 2016)that state players of GWAPs and citizen science games are motivated to play the game to help science. Moreover, based on the Motivations, Learning and Creativity model (Jennett et al., 2016), one of the initial motivators to play a citizen science game is their interest in science. Another participant said she would try the game despite finding the introduction unappealing. P6 (Text) mentioned that she would play the game due to her being interested in word games. However, she would like a more *"appealing"* interface from the first screen. Despite aesthetics not being the primary motivator for players to play a GWAP, presenting an attractive interface can still boost user engagement (Bui et al., 2020; Wang et al., 2015).

5.1.2. Large Chunks of Text Overwhelms Players

Players who were introduced to the text version of the onboarding found that the initial screens could be improved by adding visuals. In fact, they were taken aback by the text and would skip over information. This may cause future issues to arise in gameplay, as skipping over instructions might result in them missing vital information about the game. *"I am used to seeing more than a couple of sentences in one block of text and just skipping it."* says P2 (Text). Skipping the instruction could confuse players later on when they need it. One participant (P6, Text) described it as *"boring."* This could be due to the text version looking unappealing. Splitting text into several slides helped some players reduce their cognitive load. For instance, P4 (Text) found it easy to read the story because it was divided into different slides instead of presenting the text all on one screen. However, despite splitting the text up, some players still found the story too long. P9 (Text) mentioned that because games are played for fun, she does not think anyone will have time to read a long story. Another player (P10, Text) brought up that while the story seems *"complex"* and *"wordy"*, it is not an issue once you get into the game.

When participants were asked how they would improve the introduction, one player (P10, Text) replied, *"Pictures [would improve the onboarding screen]. I would maybe have a few diagrams to break it up a bit. Just so you don't get lost in the text."* This suggestion by the player allows us to understand that presenting too much textual information without the use of any graphics can overwhelm players. Likewise, one (P9, Text) player explained why she would prefer seeing visuals presented during the onboarding as it is more *"catchy"*. When asked to explain why she answered:

"When it is a picture, it will just go into the mind rather than when reading [it]. So once they see [the pictures], they will be able to understand and then they will just jump into the game." (P9, Text)

This notion is supported by the Dual Coding theory (Paivio, 1971), which suggests visuals along with text could help users recall and recognise faster than instructions without visuals. Another participant (P2, Text) suggests adding visuals to assist her in learning in-game tasks:

"[Adding] visuals in with the text helps me kind of like, put together what I will then see in the game with what I'm learning about. I'll remember more easily what the things are like and what I can do with the certain buildings." (P2, Text)

To conclude this section, when text is presented along with visuals in the onboarding phase, information retrieval is improved, and players are not required to use up too much energy processing information. Thus, allowing players to feel engaged when interacting with the game interface.

5.2. Instructions Lack Linguistic Context

In the previous section, we found that players were not interested when large chunks of text were being presented. However, in this section, players needed more guidance and instructions, specifically on linguistic tasks. Players found the instructions of the overall game clear; however, the instructions of the game failed to connect with linguistic tasks found in the mini-games. While the tutorial was understandable and clear, it did not dive into linguistic concepts. Lacking an explanation of those linguistic concepts will negatively impact the player later in the game. When the tutorial lacks sufficient instructions, the player is put under extraneous load. This ultimately leads to the player experiencing frustration. (Miller and Cooper, 2022) study found that most issues were found in the onboarding phase of citizen science games as they failed to explain critical scientific concepts to players. While the onboarding phase in this study did not provide players with linguistic concepts, the players found the general instructions simple enough to follow:

"[The tutorial] was definitely very easy to understand. The text was very simplistic, and easy to read. Wasn't very long, so it wasn't overwhelming." (P7, Animation)

Likewise, P5 (Animation) described the instructions and tutorial as *"straightforward"* and *"clear"*. Ensuring that instructions are kept brief is one of the heuristics that (van der Meij, 1995) proposed for designing minimalist instructions. Adopting these principles and heuristics was found to increase engagement in the onboarding phase of an application (Strahm et al., 2018). However, while the instructions are simple and illustrate to the player the main objectives of the game, they fail to give adequate information on the linguistic tasks:

"It doesn't tell me what I'm going to have to do. It doesn't even give me a hint [...] It's not informative. As far as the tasks that I'm going to have to perform in the game, you know, I still have no idea what I'm going to be doing." (P12, Animation)

Due to the tutorial lacking sufficient instructions, the player is put under extraneous load, causing them to feel frustrated. Thus, reducing engagement and decreasing the players' learning efficiency (Sweller, 2011). A widely used theory to explain this player's experience is the Cognitive Load Theory, which has been frequently used in-game research (Huang and Johnson, 2009) to influence the design of instructional information. Similar to Miller and Cooper (2022) study, the instructions presented in the onboarding phase failed to introduce high-level concepts to players. Based on Reigeluth's elaboration theory (Reigeluth and Stein, 1983), high-level concepts should be presented alongside sub-concepts to teach instructions effectively.

In the onboarding phase of the game, players were only given information on sub-concepts, such as instructions relating to the gameplay. Like the elaboration theory, Van Merriënboer and Kirschner (2017) proposed the Four-Component Instructional Design model, which highlighted the need to introduce whole tasks rather than solely focusing on smaller tasks. Players need to be introduced to the linguistic tasks of the game to understand the gameplay entirely. Similar to the comments expressed by P12 (Animation), P9 (Text) mentioned the lack of linguistic concepts found in the onboarding phase:

"I'm yet to understand what is the basic concept we are trying to do, actually. I don't have much idea about what you are trying to do with linguistics." (P9, Text)

When players cannot understand the tasks that they initially joined the game to do, they look for hints. An example of that is when P4 (Text) looked at the titles of the mini-games to get a hint on what she will be doing. She felt like they did not provide her with any information on the game. When reading the tutorial instruction, she concluded that PhraseFarms is a game relating to the use of phrases. However, the other two games, WordClicker and Lingotorium did not give the player clear information on what to do. The player's assumption was incorrect; this indicates that she was not presented with sufficient information. Players should be presented with the information they seek to avoid players guessing tasks and experiencing frustrations when those tasks are incorrect.

Lastly, despite most players expecting more information about linguistic concepts to be presented early on, some participants were not concerned with the linguistic context not being explained in the tutorial. Instead, they expect to be presented with more instructions later in the mini-games:

"I think they [instructions] are fine, to be honest, as long as when you get to PhraseFarm or when you get to the cafe clicker or the bakery, it's clearer on what you need to do at that point, then that's fine." (P10, Text)

Similarly, another player explained how remembering instructions that are not needed could be cognitively difficult and unnecessary. Those instructions should instead be presented at an appropriate time:

"It didn't go into detail as to what those tasks were going to be. But I presume that if you were to go into the building, that it would explain each one in detail, and I don't think it's necessary to explain it at the beginning because I just don't think you would remember [...] remembering the parts that it did talk about is probably enough at that stage of the game." (P7, Animation)

Gee (2003) suggests introducing game mechanics when the player must utilise them. Context-sensitive tutorials display contextually relevant information to the user. In contrast, context-insensitive tutorials provide all the information up front regardless of the context. This indicates that a context-sensitive tutorial could be helpful in giving players information when they need it, especially in a GWAP (Andersen et al., 2012).

5.3. Tutorial and Game Interface Requires Refinement

At last, we discovered many usability issues associated with the onboarding phase and the general game interface. A lack of usability can ultimately hinder a state of flow. For this reason, it is crucial to address those usability issues. Overall, the game interface seems easy to navigate but lacks necessary feedback. This includes feedback that can direct and assist the user in completing the tutorial and feedback that helps the player avoid mistakes. Another issue that many players have commented on is related to the graphics found in the game, which include the icons representing the mini-games. In GWAPs, UI and technical issues are commonly found, hindering player learnability (Miller and Cooper, 2022). Therefore it is vital to identify those issues and find the appropriate design solutions.

5.3.1. Tutorial Feedback is Unsupportive

Feedback is an essential component used to promote the usability of user interfaces; it is commonly featured in usability heuristics (Nielsen, 1994; Shneiderman et al., 2016). However, the wrong kind of feedback can negatively affect a user's experience. For instance, visual cues help players navigate through the game. Presenting visual cues such as icons, labels, and buttons on the map calls the player to action guiding players on what to do. When a player understands the system's current state, the gulf of execution is small (Norman, 1986). An example of this is when a player is presented with a design that supports the heuristic visibility of system status (Nielsen, 1994). Visual cues need to accurately represent the goal as they can signal to the players that an action is available for them to take:

"I like the fact that it highlights the buildings when you hover over it, so it recognises that and you know, it's very clear that there was an action there. There's something for me to do" (P10, Text)

This suggests that giving the user a visual cue assists in directing the players to the correct actions. However, visual cues can be misused and affect the game's usability. An example of this is when P11 (Animation) clicked on the town icon and expected the town icon to disappear. The interface gives a call to action to the wrong action causing the player to feel confused:

"I would have expected that like this play now tutorial town would have changed or gone away or because at first I was like, Wait, did it work when I clicked on it? You know? But now I'm seeing that since these are lighting up that it seems like there are now more options available to me." (P11, Animation)

Another player P10 (Text), thought the icons presenting the tutorial town should not be visible before completing the tutorial. Instead, the icons should appear when the player is ready to begin the game. Designers must be cautious when presenting them as presenting the incorrect visual cues can result in a player making a mistake. P5 (Animation) finds it confusing that some buildings are being highlighted when hovered over despite her not finishing the tutorial. She further explains, *"it looks like you can immediately go to them"*. Additionally, if a wrong action is made, the corrective feedback is lacking:

"I found it odd that when I clicked on the wrong thing, [the map] just zoomed out, and it didn't highlight or indicate the bakery or anything [...] So if it goes wrong, maybe some indicators like nudge [you] towards where you need to be?" (P5, Animation)

When a user executes a wrong action, the system must provide adequate feedback. This is supported by the 'Help users recognise, diagnose, and recover from errors' heuristic proposed by (Nielsen, 1994). Moreover, providing feedback promotes learnability. According to an instructional design model (Van Merriënboer and Kester, 2014), feedback correcting wrong actions is essential to achieving learning.

5.3.2. Graphics are Unclear

The game's aesthetics is very subjective, as some players prefer one style over the other. For instance, one participant (P10, Text) liked the simpler graphics, *"I liked the graphics. I like the fact they're not overly complex"*. While others expected more game assets to be present, P7 (Animation) suggested improving the trees, grass, and adding *"little features, just to make it a little bit more appealing to the eye."* Similarly, P9 (Text) expected to see more features, such as buildings, present on the map. Taking it a step further, P1 (Text) suggested adding animations on the map to make it lively:

"So it'd be the sort of thing where I'd want to like zoom in and out and try to see what was happening or maybe some small animations of people running between buildings [...] even if it's just repeated [animations] of people going from building to building carrying things" (P1, Text)

Improving the aesthetics of a game has been shown to enhance engagement in GWAPs (Wang et al., 2015; Bui et al., 2020). However, our primary focus is on the usability of the game, thus, we need to ensure the players can easily navigate around the game's interface. P7 (Animation) mentioned that the game map is clear and easy to navigate:

"In terms of just the general layout, it's very simple. It's very easy to navigate. I think somebody of any age could easily figure out this game. So I think it's pretty obvious. There's not also much else going on on the screen. It's a very, like, clean screen minus the town icon. So I would have no problem [navigating]." (P7,

Animation)

Despite P7 (Animation) finding the game easy to figure out when she first was introduced to the map, she later mentioned that the some buildings are easier to distinguish than others:

"The bakery is the least obvious one. I would have had to look to the farm and the library first to realise that that was the bakery. Because yeah, now that I see it, I see like a little bakery written on it. Because I remembered the three buildings [in the tutorial], I was able to realise like, okay, that must be the bakery. But the farm and the library are more obvious to recognise." (P7, Animation)

In the quote above, P7 (Animation) refers to the tutorial where each building was presented visually. Even though she found the bakery the least obvious of the three, she thought it was easy to find which building was because she recognised them from the tutorial. This indicates a benefit to presenting visuals in the tutorial as they help players recognise objects found on the map. However, providing more explicit labels of the icons on the map can still be necessary for those who experienced the animated onboarding phase. For example, P12 (Animation) adds that players could face difficulties remembering and distinguishing buildings in the game:

"I'm not sure that people who play the game will remember which is which, in the end. I mean, the icons are similar enough [...] they're not very distinguishable. Right. So like, I know, the one at the bottom left is the farm and the one. Above the tutorial town is the bakery. I know that but I may very well forget it [...] the work that I'm doing could interfere with my playing the game. I mean, there's already like, there's a lot of executive tasks involved." (P12, Animation)

The 'executive tasks' that P12 (Animation) mentioned could refer to the tasks related to executive functions, such as using one's working memory. This is not ideal in a game as it can lead to extraneous cognitive load. Another player, P1 (Text), mentioned that he was *"struggling"* to figure out which of the buildings, further supporting previous comments that the buildings are hard to distinguish. A solution to this is to follow Nielsen (1994) 'Recognise instead of recall' principle to minimise the memory load on the player. According to Dual Coding theory, presenting both text and visuals to a player will allow players to retrieve information quicker (Paivio, 1971). For example, this can be done by adding labels to the icons found on the map. The issue with the building icons was primarily present with the 'bakery' building when compared to the other buildings:

"hard to see the word bakery on the building, ah, hard to recognise the bakery, the farm in the library stood out, but I just knew Bakery was supposed to be there and then I couldn't see the word bakery." (P8, Animation).

Despite P8 (Animation) being introduced to the game through the animated onboarding phase, it was still difficult for her to recall the bakery building because the label was unclear. P4 (Text) also found that the bakery label was unreadable. Furthermore, some players recommended making changes to solve the issue found in the 'bakery' building. For instance, P9 (Text) recommended making the bakery building more obvious because she found that it is difficult to distinguish the different buildings. Another design suggestion made by a player is to separate the label from the building. P4 (Text) suggested that instead of having the titles of the game directly on the building, it can instead be *"be written separately like bigger and more in a clearer way in order to easily find [the building]"*. Similar to P4 (text), P11 suggested adding labels to the building icons:

"It might be helpful if like a name for these would pop up I mean, like I can see that's a barn, this does say bakery but something like this you know like little text underneath would help me understand like what each of and also remind me because I know like in that little introduction blurb it said like you can play such and such mini-game in this place and this game in that place. Having those reminders here might be helpful like when I mouse over each one" (P11, Animation)

Based on the players' design recommendations, players would prefer recognising instead of recalling icons regardless of which presentation of the onboarding phase they were presented with. Finally, applying the design recommendations suggested by players could refine and improve the onboarding phase of the game.

6. Conclusion and Future Work

Based on our findings, most of the players presented with the text version wanted animations or visuals, while some players who were presented with the animation found it was 'standard' to be presented with an animation in the introduction of the game but missing sound. Despite that, players who viewed the animation gave positive feedback on the animation. Participants who were presented with the text version found the text overwhelming and dull, lacking visuals. The narrative interested both groups, and the instructions were clear in both versions. However, despite the instructions being clear, some participants would skip over large chunks of text or fail to remember some information. Unfortunately, the onboarding phase lacked linguistic context making it difficult for players to understand their purpose for playing the game. Additionally, the usability issues found in the tutorial and game interface hindered player engagement. We conclude that while the presentation format of the onboarding phase does affect player engagement, other aspects of the onboarding phase can play a role in player engagement and should be further explored.

7. Bibliographical References

Andersen, E., O'Rourke, E., Liu, Y.-E., Snider, R., Lowdermilk, J., Truong, D., Cooper, S., and Popovic, Z. (2012). The impact of tutorials on games of varying complexity. In *Proceedings of the SIGCHI Conference on Human Factors in Computing Systems*, CHI '12, pages 59–68, New York, NY, USA, May. Association for Computing Machinery.

Bouta, H. and Retalis, S. (2013). Enhancing primary school children collaborative learning experiences in maths via a 3D virtual environment. *Education and Information Technologies*, 18(4):571–596, December.

Bowser, A., Hansen, D., He, Y., Boston, C., Reid, M., Gunnell, L., and Preece, J. (2013). Using gamification to inspire new citizen science volunteers. In *Proceedings of the First International Conference on Gameful Design, Research, and Applications*, Gamification '13, pages 18–25, New York, NY, USA, October. Association for Computing Machinery.

Boyle, E. A., Hainey, T., Connolly, T. M., Gray, G., Earp, J., Ott, M., Lim, T., Ninaus, M., Ribeiro, C., and Pereira, J. (2016). An update to the systematic literature review of empirical evidence of the impacts and outcomes of computer games and serious games. *Comput. Educ.*, 94:178–192, March.

Braun, V. and Clarke, V. (2021). One size fits all? what counts as quality practice in (reflexive) thematic analysis? *Qual. Res. Psychol.*, 18(3):328–352, July.

Bui, P., Rodríguez-Aflecht, G., Brezovszky, B., Hannula-Sormunen, M. M., Laato, S., and Lehtinen, E. (2020). Understanding students' game experiences throughout the developmental process of the number navigation game.

Causer, T. W. (2012). Building a volunteer community: Results and findings from transcribe bentham.

Cheung, G. K., Zimmermann, T., and Nagappan, N. (2014). The first hour experience: how the initial play can engage (or lose) new players. In *Proceedings of the first ACM SIGCHI annual symposium on Computer-human interaction in play*, CHI PLAY '14, pages 57–66, New York, NY, USA, October. Association for Computing Machinery.

Chou, Y.-K. (2019). *Actionable Gamification: Beyond Points, Badges, and Leaderboards*. Packt Publishing Ltd, December.

Crowston, K. and Prestopnik, N. R. (2013). Motivation and data quality in a citizen science game: A design science evaluation. In *2013 46th Hawaii International Conference on System Sciences*, pages 450–459. ieeexplore.ieee.org, January.

Csikszentmihalyi, M. (1990). *Flow: The psychology of optimal experience*, volume 1990. Harper & Row New York.

Curtis, V. (2015). Motivation to participate in an online citizen science game: A study of foldit. *Sci. Commun.*, 37(6):723–746, December.

de Leon Pereira, R., Tan, A., Bunt, A., and Tremblay-Savard, O. (2021). Increasing player engagement, retention and performance through the inclusion of educational content in a citizen science game. In *The 16th International Conference on the Foundations of Digital Games (FDG) 2021*, number Article 16 in FDG'21, pages 1–12, New York, NY, USA, August. Association for Computing Machinery.

Doherty, K. and Doherty, G. (2018). Engagement in HCI: Conception, theory and measurement. *ACM Comput. Surv.*, 51(5):1–39, November.

Eveleigh, A., Jennett, C., Blandford, A., Brohan, P., and Cox, A. L. (2014). Designing for dabblers and deterring drop-outs in citizen science. In *Proceedings of the SIGCHI Conference on Human Factors in Computing Systems*, CHI '14, pages 2985–2994, New York, NY, USA, April. Association for Computing Machinery.

Fort, K., Guillaume, B., and Chastant, H. (2014). Creating zombilingo, a game with a purpose for dependency syntax annotation. In *Proceedings of the First International Workshop on Gamification for Information Retrieval*, GamifIR '14, page 2–6, New York, NY, USA. Association for Computing Machinery.

Gee, J. P. (2003). What video games have to teach us about learning and literacy. *Computers in entertainment (CIE)*, 1(1):20–20.

Greenhill, A., Holmes, K., Woodcock, J., Lintott, C., Simmons, B. D., Graham, G., Cox, J., Young, O. E., and Masters, K. (2016). Playing with science: Exploring how game activity motivates users participation on an online citizen science platform. *Aslib Journal of Information Management*, 68(3):306–325, January.

Guillaume, B., Fort, K., and Lefebvre, N. (2016). Crowdsourcing complex language resources: Playing to annotate dependency syntax. In *International Conference on Computational Linguistics (COLING)*. hal.inria.fr.

Hamari, J. and Keronen, L. (2017). Why do people play games? a meta-analysis. *Int. J. Inf. Manage.*, 37(3):125–141, June.

Hawlitschek, A. and Joeckel, S. (2017). Increasing the effectiveness of digital educational games: The effects of a learning instruction on students' learning, motivation and cognitive load. *Comput. Human Behav.*, 72:79–86, July.

Huang, W. D. and Johnson, T. (2009). Instructional game design using cognitive load theory.

Hunicke, R., LeBlanc, M., and Zubek, R. (2004). MDA: A formal approach to game design and game research. In *Proceedings of the AAAI Workshop on Challenges in Game AI*, volume 4, page 1722.

Iacovides, I., Jennett, C., Cornish-Trestrail, C., and Cox, A. L. (2013). Do games attract or sustain engagement in citizen science? a study of volunteer motivations. In *CHI '13 Extended Abstracts on Human Factors in Computing Systems*, CHI EA '13, pages 1101–1106, New York, NY, USA, April. Association for Computing Machinery.

Islas Sedano, C., Leendertz, V., Vinni, M., Sutinen, E., and Ellis, S. (2013). Hypercontextualized learning games: Fantasy, motivation, and engagement in reality. *Simul. Gaming*, 44(6):821–845, December.

Jennett, C., Kloetzer, L., Schneider, D., Iacovides, I., Cox, A., Gold, M., Fuchs, B., Eveleigh, A., Methieu, K., Ajani, Z., and Talsi, Y. (2016). Motivations, learning and creativity in online citizen science. *Journal of Science Communication*, 15(3), April.

Kicikoglu, D., Bartle, R., Chamberlain, J., and Poesio, M. (2019). Wormingo. In *Proceedings of the 14th International Conference on the Foundations of Digital Games*, New York, NY, USA, August. ACM.

Kirschner, P. A. (2002). Cognitive load theory: implications of cognitive load theory on the design of learning. *Learning and Instruction*, 12(1):1–10, February.

Lafourcade, M., Joubert, A., and Le Brun, N. (2015). *Games with a Purpose (GWAPS)*. John Wiley & Sons.

Lafourcade, M. (2007). Making people play for lexical acquisition with the JeuxDeMots prototype. In *SNLP'07: 7th international symposium on natural language processing*, page 7.

Lewis, C. (1982). *Using the" thinking-aloud" method in cognitive interface design*. IBM TJ Watson Research Center Yorktown Heights.

Madge, C., Chamberlain, J., Kruschwitz, U., and Poesio, M. (2017). Experiment-driven development of a gwap for marking segments in text. In *Extended Abstracts Publication of the Annual Symposium on Computer-Human Interaction in Play*, pages 397–404.

Madge, C., Bartle, R., Chamberlain, J., Kruschwitz, U., and Poesio, M. (2019). Incremental game mechanics applied to text annotation. In *Proceedings of the Annual Symposium on Computer-Human Interaction in Play*, pages 545–558.

Malone, T. W. and Lepper, M. R. (1987). Making learning fun: A taxonomy of intrinsic motivations for learning. In *Aptitude, learning, and instruction*, pages 223–254. Routledge.

Malone, T. W. (1982). Heuristics for designing enjoyable user interfaces: Lessons from computer games. In *Proceedings of the 1982 conference on Human factors in computing systems*, pages 63–68.

Mayer, R. E. and Moreno, R. (2002). Animation as an aid to multimedia learning. *Educ. Psychol. Rev.*, 14(1):87–99, March.

Mekler, E. D., Tuch, A. N., Martig, A. L., and Opwis, K. (2014). A diary study exploring game completion and player experience. In *Proceedings of the first ACM SIGCHI annual symposium on Computer-human interaction in play*, CHI PLAY '14, pages 433–434, New York, NY, USA, October. Association for Computing Machinery.

Mildner, P., Stamer, N., and Effelsberg, W. (2015). From game characteristics to effective learning games. In *Serious Games*, pages 51–62. Springer International Publishing.

Miller, J. A. and Cooper, S. (2022). Barriers to expertise in citizen science games. In *CHI Conference on Human Factors in Computing Systems*, pages 1–25.

Miller, J. A., Narayan, U., Hantsbarger, M., Cooper, S., and El-Nasr, M. S. (2019). Expertise and engagement: Re-Designing citizen science games with players' minds in mind. *FDG*, 2019, August.

Nielsen, J. (1994). *Usability Engineering*. Morgan Kaufmann, October.

Norman, D. A. (1986). Cognitive engineering. *User centered system design*, 31:61.

Novak, E. (2015). A critical review of digital storyline-enhanced learning. *Educational Technology Research and Development*, 63(3):431–453.

Paivio, A. (1971). Imagery and language. In *Imagery*, pages 7–32. Elsevier.

Palmiter, S. and Elkerton, J. (1993). Animated demonstrations for learning procedural Computer-Based tasks. *Human–Computer Interaction*, 8(3):193–216, September.

Palmiter, S., Elkerton, J., and Baggett, P. (1991). Animated demonstrations vs written instructions for learning procedural tasks: a preliminary investigation. *Int. J. Man. Mach. Stud.*, 34(5):687–701, May.

Poesio, M., Chamberlain, J., Kruschwitz, U., Robaldo, L., and Ducceschi, L. (2013). Phrase detectives: Utilizing collective intelligence for internet-scale language resource creation. *ACM Trans. Interact. Intell. Syst.*, 3(1):1–44, April.

Prestopnik, N. R. and Tang, J. (2015). Points, stories, worlds, and diegesis: Comparing player experiences in two citizen science games. *Comput. Human Behav.*, 52:492–506, November.

Raddick, M. J., Bracey, G., Carney, K., Gyuk, G., Borne, K., Wallin, J., Jacoby, S., and Planetarium, A. (2009). Citizen science: status and research directions for the coming decade. *AGB Stars and Related Phenomenastro 2010: The Astronomy and Astrophysics Decadal Survey*, 2010:46P.

Reigeluth, C. and Stein, R. (1983). Elaboration theory. *Instructional-design theories and models: An overview of their current status (1983)*, pages 335–381.

Segundo Díaz, R. L., Rovelo Ruiz, G., Bouzouita, M., and Coninx, K. (2022). Building blocks for creating enjoyable games—a systematic literature review. *Int. J. Hum.-Comput. Stud.*, 159(C), March.

Shelley, B. (2001). Guidelines for developing successful games. *Gamasutra (August 2001), http://www. gamasutra. com.*

Shneiderman, B., Plaisant, C., Cohen, M. S., Jacobs, S., Elmqvist, N., and Diakopoulos, N. (2016). *De-*

signing the user interface: strategies for effective human-computer interaction. Pearson.

Strahm, B., Gray, C. M., and Vorvoreanu, M. (2018). Generating mobile application onboarding insights through minimalist instruction. In *Proceedings of the 2018 Designing Interactive Systems Conference*, DIS '18, pages 361–372, New York, NY, USA, June. Association for Computing Machinery.

Sweller, J. (2011). CHAPTER TWO - cognitive load theory. In Jose P Mestre et al., editors, *Psychology of Learning and Motivation*, volume 55, pages 37–76. Academic Press, January.

Tinati, R., Luczak-Roesch, M., Simperl, E., and Hall, W. (2017). An investigation of player motivations in eyewire, a gamified citizen science project. *Comput. Human Behav.*, 73:527–540, August.

van der Meij, H. (1995). Principles and heuristics for designing minimalist instruction. *Technical Communication*, 42(2):243–261.

Van Merriënboer, J. J. and Kester, L. (2014). The four-component instructional design model: Multimedia principles in environments for complex learning.

Van Merriënboer, J. J. G. and Kirschner, P. A. (2017). *Ten steps to complex learning: A systematic approach to four-component instructional design*. Routledge.

Von Ahn, L. and Dabbish, L. (2004). Labeling images with a computer game. In *Proceedings of the SIGCHI conference on Human factors in computing systems*, pages 319–326.

Wang, X., Goh, D. H.-L., Lim, E.-P., and Vu, A. W. L. (2015). Aesthetic experience and acceptance of human computation games. In *Digital Libraries: Providing Quality Information*, pages 264–273. Springer International Publishing.

Zubek, R. (2020). *Elements of Game Design*. MIT Press, August.

Zyngier, D. (2008). (re)conceptualising student engagement: Doing education not doing time. *Teaching and Teacher Education*, 24(7):1765–1776, October.

Proceedings of the 9th Games and Natural Language Processing Workshop @LREC2022, pages 28–39
Marseille, 25 June 2022

NLU for Game-based Learning in Real: Initial Evaluations

Eda Okur, Saurav Sahay, Lama Nachman
Intel Labs
USA
{eda.okur, saurav.sahay, lama.nachman}@intel.com

Abstract

Intelligent systems designed for play-based interactions should be contextually aware of the users and their surroundings. Spoken Dialogue Systems (SDS) are critical for these interactive agents to carry out effective goal-oriented communication with users in real-time. For the real-world (i.e., in-the-wild) deployment of such conversational agents, improving the Natural Language Understanding (NLU) module of the goal-oriented SDS pipeline is crucial, especially with limited task-specific datasets. This study explores the potential benefits of a recently proposed transformer-based multi-task NLU architecture, mainly to perform Intent Recognition on small-size domain-specific educational game datasets. The evaluation datasets were collected from children practicing basic math concepts via play-based interactions in game-based learning settings. We investigate the NLU performances on the initial proof-of-concept game datasets versus the real-world deployment datasets and observe anticipated performance drops in-the-wild. We have shown that compared to the more straightforward baseline approaches, Dual Intent and Entity Transformer (DIET) architecture (Bunk et al., 2020) is robust enough to handle real-world data to a large extent for the Intent Recognition task on these domain-specific in-the-wild game datasets.

Keywords: Spoken Dialogue Systems, Natural Language Understanding, Intent Recognition, Game-based Learning

1. Introduction

Investigating Artificial Intelligence (AI) systems that can help children in their learning process has been a challenging yet exciting area of research (Chassignol et al., 2018; Zhai et al., 2021). Utilizing Natural Language Processing (NLP) for building educational games and applications has gained popularity in the past decade (Lende and Raghuwanshi, 2016; Cahill et al., 2020). Game-based learning systems can offer significant advantages in teaching fundamental math concepts interactively, especially for younger students (Skene et al., 2022). These intelligent systems are often required to handle multimodal understanding of the kids and their surroundings in real-time. Spoken Dialogue Systems (SDS) are vital building blocks for efficient task-oriented communication with children in game-based learning settings. In this study, the application domain is a multimodal dialogue system for younger kids learning basic math concepts through gamified interactions. Such dialogue system technology needs to be constructed and modeled carefully to handle task-oriented game interactions between the children and a virtual character serving as a conversational agent.

Building the Natural Language Understanding (NLU) module of a goal-oriented SDS for game-based interactions usually involves: (i) the definition of intents (and entities if needed); (ii) creation of game-specific and task-relevant datasets; (iii) annotation of the game data with domain-specific intents and entities; (iv) iterative training and evaluation of NLU models; (v) repeating this tedious process for every new or updated game usages. Improving the NLU performances of task-oriented SDS pipelines in low-data regimes is quite challenging. This study primarily explores the potential benefits of a recent transformer-based multi-task architecture proposed for joint Intent and Entity Recognition tasks, especially with limited game datasets. Utilizing that flexible architecture, we focus on increasing the performance of our NLU models trained on small-size task-specific game datasets. The main NLU task we aim to improve is the Intent Recognition from possible user/player utterances during gamified learning interactions. Given an input utterance, the goal of an Intent Recognition model is to predict the user's intent (e.g., what the player wants to accomplish within a game-based interaction).

This work investigates the Intent Recognition model performances on our early proof-of-concept (POC) educational game datasets created to bootstrap the SDS to be deployed later in the real world. We have shown that adopting the recently proposed lightweight Dual Intent and Entity Transformer (DIET) architecture (Bunk et al., 2020) along with the Conversational Representations from Transformers (ConveRT) embeddings (Henderson et al., 2020) is a promising approach for NLU. This method boosts the NLU performance results on our initial small-scale POC game datasets. After the exploratory validation studies were conducted in-the-lab, the final evaluation datasets were collected in-the-wild from students working on fundamental math concepts in a game-based learning space at school. We examine the Intent Recognition performances on these real-world deployment datasets and reveal highly expected performance degradations in-the-wild. Compared to the baseline approaches, we have shown that adopting a DIET classifier with pre-trained ConveRT representations still achieves improved NLU results on our evaluation datasets collected in-the-wild.

2. Related Work

The use of AI technologies to enhance students' learning experiences has gained increasing popularity, especially in the last decade (Chassignol et al., 2018; Aslan et al., 2019; Jia et al., 2020; Baker, 2021; Zhai et al., 2021; Zhang and Aslan, 2021). Intelligent game-based learning systems (Lester et al., 2013; Richey et al., 2021) present significant benefits for practicing math concepts in smart spaces (Pires et al., 2019; Sun et al., 2021), specifically for early childhood education (Skene et al., 2022). Adapting NLP techniques to build various educational applications has been an appealing area of research for quite some time (Meurers, 2012; Blanchard et al., 2015; Lende and Raghuwanshi, 2016; Taghipour and Ng, 2016; Raamadhurai et al., 2019; Cahill et al., 2020; Ghosh et al., 2020). To slightly narrow down on these applications, building conversational agents for the smart education has been widely studied in the community (Graesser et al., 2004; Litman and Silliman, 2004; Kerry et al., 2009; Roos, 2018; Winkler and Söllner, 2018; Palasundram et al., 2019; Winkler et al., 2020). Relatively few number of studies also exist specifically on recognizing goals or intents of players in educational games (Min et al., 2016; Min et al., 2017; Hooshyar et al., 2019).

Since our ultimate goal is to build dialogue systems for interactive educational games, we have outlined the previous studies with applications of AI and NLP for education context until now (e.g., intelligent systems and conversational agents for play-based learning). Next, we will briefly summarize the dialogue system technologies and NLU approaches in a more generic context.

Dialogue systems are frequently categorized as either task-oriented or open-ended. The task-oriented dialogue systems are designed to fulfill specific tasks and handle goal-oriented conversations. The open-ended systems or chatbots, on the other hand, allow more generic conversations such as chit-chat (Jurafsky and Martin, 2018). With the advancements of deep learning-based language technologies and increased availability of large datasets with computing power in the research community, the dialogue systems trained end-to-end produce promising results for both goal-oriented (Bordes et al., 2017) and open-ended (Dodge et al., 2016) applications. Dialogue Managers (DM) of goal-oriented systems are often sequential decision-making models. The optimal policies can be learned via reinforcement learning from a high number of user interactions (Shah et al., 2016; Dhingra et al., 2017; Liu et al., 2017; Su et al., 2017; Cuayáhuitl, 2017). Unfortunately, building such systems with limited user interactions is extremely challenging. Therefore, supervised learning approaches with modular SDS pipelines are still widely preferred when initial training data is limited, basically to bootstrap the goal-oriented conversational agents for further data collection (Sahay et al., 2019). Statistical and neural network-based dialogue system toolkits and frameworks (Bocklisch et al., 2017; Ultes et al., 2017; Burtsev et al., 2018) are heavily used in the academic and industrial research communities for implicit dialogue context management.

The NLU module within SDS pipeline processes the user utterances as input and often predicts the user intents (along with entities of interest if necessary). LSTM networks (Hochreiter and Schmidhuber, 1997) and Bidirectional LSTMs (Schuster and Paliwal, 1997) have been widely utilized for sequence learning tasks such as Intent Classification and Slot Filling (Mesnil et al., 2015; Hakkani-Tür et al., 2016). Joint training of Intent Recognition and Entity Extraction models have been explored recently (Zhang and Wang, 2016; Liu and Lane, 2016; Goo et al., 2018; Varghese et al., 2020). Several hierarchical multi-task architectures are proposed for these joint NLU approaches (Zhou et al., 2016; Wen et al., 2018; Okur et al., 2019; Vanzo et al., 2019), few of them in multimodal context (Gu et al., 2017; Okur et al., 2020). Vaswani et al. (2017) proposed the Transformer as a novel neural network architecture based entirely on attention mechanisms (Bahdanau et al., 2015). Shortly after, Bidirectional Encoder Representations from Transformers (BERT) (Devlin et al., 2019) became one of the significant breakthroughs in pre-trained language representations, showing strong performance in numerous NLP tasks, including the NLU. Recently, Bunk et al. (2020) introduced the Dual Intent and Entity Transformer (DIET) as a lightweight multi-task architecture that outperforms fine-tuning BERT for predicting intents and entities on a complex multi-domain NLU-Benchmark dataset (Liu et al., 2021). On the efficient representation learning side, Henderson et al. (2020) lately proposed the Conversational Representations from Transformers (ConveRT), which is also a lightweight approach to obtain pre-trained embeddings as sentence representations to be successfully utilized in numerous conversational AI tasks.

3. NLU Models

This section describes the models we examine for the NLU (i.e., Intent Recognition) module within a dialogue system pipeline. We have built our NLU models on top of the Rasa open-source framework (Bocklisch et al., 2017). The former baseline Intent Recognition architecture available in Rasa is based on supervised embeddings provided within the Rasa NLU (Bocklisch et al., 2017), which is an embedding-based text classifier that embeds user utterances and intent labels into the same vector space. This former baseline architecture is inspired by the StarSpace work (Wu et al., 2018), where the supervised embeddings are trained by maximizing the similarity between intents and utterances. The algorithm learns to represent user inputs and intents into a common embedding space and compares them against each other in that vectorial space. It also learns to rank a set of intents given a user utterance and

Figure 1: Learning basic math via game play-based interactions.

provides similarity rankings of these labels. In Sahay et al. (2019), the authors enriched this embedding-based former baseline Rasa Intent Classifier by incorporating additional features and adapting alternative network architectures. To be more precise, they adapted the Transformer network (Vaswani et al., 2017) and incorporated pre-trained BERT embeddings using the `bert-base-uncased` model (Devlin et al., 2019) to improve the Intent Recognition performance. In this work, we employed this improved approach from Sahay et al. (2019) as our baseline NLU model, which we would call TF+BERT in our experiments.

In this study, we explore the potential improvements in Intent Classification performance by adapting the recent DIET architecture (Bunk et al., 2020). DIET is a transformer-based multi-task architecture for joint Intent Recognition and Entity Extraction. It employs a 2-layer transformer shared for both of these NLU tasks. To be more precise, a sequence of entity labels is predicted with a Conditional Random Field (CRF) (Lafferty et al., 2001) tagging layer, which is on top of the transformer output sequence corresponding to the input sentences treated as a sequence of tokens. For the intent labels, the transformer output for the `__CLS__` token (i.e., classification token at the end of each sentence) and the intent labels are embedded into the same semantic vector space. The dot-product loss is utilized to maximize the similarity with the target label and minimize similarities with the negative samples. Note that DIET can incorporate pre-trained word and sentence embeddings from language models as dense features, with the flexibility to combine these with token level one-hot encodings and multi-hot encodings of character n-grams as sparse features. These sparse features are passed through a fully-connected layer with shared weights across all sequence steps. The output of this fully-connected layer is concatenated with the dense features from the pre-trained models. This flexible architecture allows us to use any pre-trained embeddings as dense features in DIET, such as GloVe (Pennington et al., 2014), BERT (Devlin et al., 2019), and ConveRT (Henderson et al., 2020).

Conversational Representations from Transformers (ConveRT) is yet another recent and promising architecture to obtain pre-trained representations that are well-suited for real-world Conversational AI applications, especially for the Intent Classification task. ConveRT is a unique transformer-based dual-encoder network leveraging quantization and subword-level parameterization. In Henderson et al. (2020), the authors show that pre-trained representations from the ConveRT sentence encoder can be transferred to the Intent Classification task with promising results. Both DIET and ConveRT are lightweight architectures with faster and memory/energy-efficient training capabilities than their counterparts. When incorporating the ConveRT embeddings with the DIET classifier, the initial embedding for `__CLS__` token is set as the input sentence encoding obtained from the ConveRT model. This way, we can leverage extra contextual information from the complete sentence on top of the word embeddings. For all the above reasons, we adapted the DIET architecture and incorporated pre-trained ConveRT embeddings to potentially improve the Intent Classification performances on our small domain-specific datasets. We would call this approach DIET+ConveRT in our experiments[1].

To investigate the actual benefits of DIET architecture versus the dense features, we also adapted DIET with out-of-the-box pre-trained BERT embeddings using the `bert-base-uncased` model (Devlin et al., 2019), as in our baseline TF+BERT NLU model. When combining these off-the-shelf BERT representations with the DIET classifier, the initial embedding for `__CLS__` token is set to the corresponding output embedding of the BERT `[CLS]` token. We would call this approach DIET+BERT in our experiments.

4. Experimental Results

4.1. Datasets

We conduct our experiments on the Kid Space Planting and Watering (PW) games NLU datasets having

[1]Please refer to Bunk et al. (2020) for hyper-parameters, hardware specifications, and computational cost details.

Statistics/Dataset	Planting Game	Watering Game
# distinct intents	14	13
total # samples (utterances)	1927	2115
min # samples per intent	22	25
max # samples per intent	555	601
avg # samples per intent	137.6	162.7
# unique words (vocab)	1314	1267
total # words	10141	10469
min # words per sample	1	1
max # words per sample	74	65
avg # words per sample	5.26	4.95

Table 1: KidSpace-PW-POC Dataset Statistics

Statistics/Dataset	Planting Game	Watering Game
# distinct intents	12	11
total # samples (utterances)	2173	2122
min # samples per intent	4	6
max # samples per intent	1005	1005
avg # samples per intent	181.1	192.9
# unique words (vocab)	772	743
total # words	10433	9508
min # words per sample	1	1
max # words per sample	45	44
avg # words per sample	4.80	4.48

Table 2: KidSpace-PW-Deployment Dataset Statistics

utterances from play-based math learning experiences designed for early school-age children (i.e., 5-to-8 years old) (Anderson et al., 2018; Aslan et al., 2022). The use-cases aim to create an interactive smart space for children with traditional gaming motivations such as level achievements and virtually collecting objects. The smart space allows multiple children to interact, which can encourage social development. The intelligent agent should accurately comprehend inputs from children and provide feedback. The AI system needs to be physically grounded to allow children to bring meaningful objects into the play experience, such as physical toys and manipulatives as learning materials. Therefore, the multimodal system would combine various sensing technologies that should interact with children, track each child, and monitor their progress.

The use-cases include a specific flow of interactive games facilitating elementary math learning. The FlowerPot game (i.e., Planting Game in Tables 1 and 2) builds on the math concepts of tens and ones, with the larger flower pots representing 'tens' and smaller pots 'ones'. The virtual character provides the number of flowers the children should plant, and when the children have placed the correct number of large and small pots against the wall, digital flowers appear. In the NumberGrid game (i.e., Watering Game in Tables 1 and 2), math clues (or questions) are presented to children. When the correct number is touched on the number grid (i.e., on the wall), water is virtually poured to water the flowers. The visual, audio, and LiDAR-based recognition technologies enable physically situated interactions. The dialogue system is expected to take multimodal information to incorporate user identity, actions, gestures, audio context, and the objects (i.e., physical manipulatives) in space. For instance, during the FlowerPot game experience, the virtual character asks the children if they are done placing pots, to which they respond 'yes' (or 'no'). The dialogue system needs to use the visual input to have the virtual character respond appropriately to the correct (or incorrect) number of pots being detected.

Figure 1 demonstrates the virtual character (i.e., Oscar the teddy bear) helping the kids with learning 'tens' and 'ones' concepts along with practicing simple counting, addition, and subtraction operations. The game datasets have a limited number of player utterances, which are manually annotated for intent types defined for each learning game or activity. For the FlowerPot game, we use the Planting Flowers game dataset, and for the NumberGrid game, we use a separate Watering Flowers game dataset. Some of the intents are quite generic across usages and games/activities (e.g., *affirm*, *deny*, *next-step*, *out-of-scope*, *goodbye*), whereas others are highly domain-dependent and game/task-specific (e.g., *intro-meadow*, *answer-flowers*, *answer-water*, *ask-number*, *answer-valid*, *answer-invalid*).

The current learning game activities are designed for two children collaboratively playing with the virtual agent. In addition to kids, an adult user (i.e., the Facilitator) is also present in the space to interact with the agent for game progress and help out the children when needed. Thus, we are dealing with a multiparty conversational system interacting with multiple users (i.e., two kids and one adult) while they progress through several learning games. In this goal-oriented dialogue system, the agent should provide the game instructions (with the Facilitator's help), guide the kids, and understand both the kids' and the Facilitator's utterances and actions to respond to them appropriately.

The NLU models are trained and validated on the initial POC datasets (Sahay et al., 2021) to bootstrap the agents for in-the-wild deployments. These POC game datasets were manually created based on the User Experience (UX) design studies to train the SDS models and then validated with the UX sessions in-the-lab with 5 kids (and one adult) going through play-based learning interactions. Table 1 shows the statistics of these KidSpace-PW-POC NLU datasets. Planting game and Watering game POC datasets have 1927 and 2115 utterances, respectively.

The deployment game datasets were later collected from 12 kids (and two adults), where the Kid Space setup was deployed in a classroom at school (Aslan et al., 2022). Table 2 shows the statistics of KidSpace-

Planting Game Datasets		# Utterances	
Type	**Intent**	**POC**	**Deployment**
Domain Specific	*intro-meadow*	23	7
	answer-flowers	110	13
	answer-valid	176	17
	answer-invalid	95	0
	intro-game	134	78
	help-affirm	41	4
	everyone-understand	22	11
	oscar-understand	25	15
	ask-number	34	18
	counting	418	581
Generic	*affirm*	144	370
	deny	125	54
	next-step	25	0
	out-of-scope	555	1005
	Total	1927	2173

Table 3: Intent Class Distributions for Planting Game

Watering Game Datasets		# Utterances	
Type	**Intent**	**POC**	**Deployment**
Domain Specific	*answer-water*	69	9
	answer-valid	201	6
	answer-invalid	91	0
	intro-game	102	30
	everyone-understand	44	11
	oscar-understand	25	15
	ask-number	73	21
	counting	476	581
Generic	*affirm*	165	370
	deny	157	54
	next-step	34	0
	out-of-scope	601	1005
	goodbye	77	20
	Total	2115	2122

Table 4: Intent Class Distributions for Watering Game

PW-Deployment NLU datasets, where Planting game and Watering game deployment datasets have 2173 and 2122 utterances, respectively. Note that these deployment datasets are used only for the testing purposes in this study, where we train our NLU models on the POC datasets. For both in-the-lab and in-the-wild datasets, the spoken user utterances are transcribed manually at first. These transcriptions are then manually annotated for the intent types we defined for each game activity. These transcribed and annotated final utterances are analyzed and used in our experiments in this study.

When we compare the POC versus deployment game datasets (in Tables 1-to- 4), we observe above 2.1k sample utterances for each game activity in both cases, except for the Planting POC data with around 1.9k samples. The number of possible user intents we envisioned for the POC was 14 and 13, respectively, for the Planting and Watering games. However, we have not observed any samples for two of the possible intent types for each game in the real-world deployment sessions. These intent types are *next-step* and *answer-invalid*, which were part of our backup intents in case we have technical issues and the users need to skip certain sub-activities (i.e., *next-step*), or in case the users provide highly irrelevant or unexpected answers to our specific questions in the game flow (i.e., *answer-invalid*). The minimum and the maximum number of samples per intent also differ significantly for the POC versus in-the-wild game datasets, which creates a huge difference in class distributions for our test samples (see Tables 3 and 4). Although we expect certain intent types to occur very infrequently in real game-plays (e.g., *help-affirm*), we still have to manually create enough samples ($\geq$20) for each intent type for the model training and validation purposes during the POC. The dominant intent class in both POC and in-the-wild datasets is *out-of-scope* (OOS). That was more or less anticipated as we are dealing with a multi-party conversational game setting here. In these games, the kids are encouraged to talk to each other while collaboratively solving the math puzzles. They can also discuss with or ask for help from the Facilitator. As the agent is in always-listening mode, if the users are not directly addressing Oscar, the system can detect those utterances as OOS (or *counting*, which is the second most frequent intent class, depending on the context). Notice that POC datasets were created with around one-fourth of the utterances as OOS, whereas the deployment datasets have almost half of the utterances tagged as OOS. That was mainly due to a relatively talkative Facilitator at school and some kids' preferences to talk to the Facilitator more often than Oscar in real deployment sessions. We have observed this behavior less often in our in-the-lab UX sessions, as the adult in the room was one of the researchers guiding kids to talk to Oscar instead. Those out-of-distribution and unseen OOS samples create additional challenges for the NLU models when tested on in-the-wild game datasets. We have also observed the vocabulary sizes shrink in-the-wild as we tried to manually curate more variations in the POC datasets to make the NLU models more robust. The average number of tokens per sample (i.e., utterance length) is around 5 in the POC data, yet, we observe slightly shorter utterances in-the-wild that might affect the available contextual information.

4.2. Intent Recognition Results

To evaluate the Intent Recognition performances, the baseline NLU model that we previously explored, TF+BERT, is compared with the DIET+BERT and DIET+ConveRT models that we adapted recently (see section 3). We conduct our evaluations on both the Planting and Watering game datasets. The models are trained and validated on the bootstrap POC datasets and then tested on the school deployment datasets. Table 5 summarizes the Intent Classification performance results on the POC datasets in micro-average

Model/Dataset	Planting Game	Watering Game
TF+BERT (Baseline)	90.50±0.25	92.43±0.32
DIET+BERT	94.00±0.38	96.39±0.14
DIET+ConveRT	**95.88±0.42**	**97.69±0.11**
Performance Gain	+5.38	+5.26

Table 5: NLU/Intent Recognition micro-avg F1-scores (%): TF+BERT, DIET+BERT, and DIET+ConveRT models trained and validated on KidSpace-PW-POC datasets (3 runs of 10-fold CV)

Model/Dataset	Planting Game	Watering Game
TF+BERT (Baseline)	85.08±0.49	90.06±0.56
DIET+BERT	87.03±0.30	89.63±0.62
DIET+ConveRT	**89.00±0.29**	**90.57±0.86**
Performance Gain	+3.92	+0.51

Table 6: NLU/Intent Recognition micro-avg F1-scores (%): TF+BERT, DIET+BERT, and DIET+ConveRT models trained on KidSpace-PW-POC (3 runs) and tested on KidSpace-PW-Deployment datasets (3 runs)

F1-scores. To test our model extensively on these limited-size POC datasets, we perform a 10-fold cross-validation (CV) by automatically creating multiple train/test splits. We report the average performance results with standard deviations obtained from the 3 runs, where we perform a 10-fold CV over the POC datasets for each run. As one can observe from Table 5, adapting the lightweight DIET architecture (Bunk et al., 2020) with pre-trained ConveRT embeddings (Henderson et al., 2020) significantly improved the Intent Classification performances for the NLU datasets manually created for POC. Specifically, the overall NLU performance gains are higher than 5% F1-scores for both Planting and Watering game datasets. Note that when we keep the dense features (i.e., pre-trained embeddings from BERT language models) constant, we can observe the clear benefits of switching from standard Transformer (TF) architecture to DIET classifier. We gain 3-to-4% F1-scores with DIET architecture, and we improve the Intent Recognition performance by another 1-to-2% with ConveRT embeddings compared to BERT. With these observations, which are consistent across different use-cases (i.e., Planting and Watering games), we updated the NLU component in our multimodal SDS pipeline by replacing the previous TF+BERT model with this promising DIET+ConveRT architecture.

Next, we investigate the NLU model performances on our real-world deployment datasets. The anticipated performance drops occurred when we tested these Intent Recognition models on in-the-wild data, which reflect more realistic game settings from a school deployment. Table 6 summarizes the Intent Classification performance results obtained on the deployment game datasets in micro-average F1-scores. Although the DIET+ConveRT models trained on POC datasets performed very well during the cross-validation (i.e., achieved around 96% and 98% F1-scores for Planting and Watering games, respectively), the performance loss is significantly high (i.e., around 7% F1-score) when tested on in-the-wild datasets. As a result, the same models achieved around 89% and 91% F1-scores when tested on the Planting and Watering deployment sets, respectively. That finding is quite common and probably not very surprising as the players in-the-wild can often largely deviate from the manual or synthetic data generation inside the labs or data collection through crowd-sourcing for interactive games. We have summarized the game dataset statistics and our preliminary observations regarding the main differences between the POC and deployment sets in section 4.1. We believe such deviations have played a significant role in the observed performance shifts for real-world play-based interactions. More specifically, the sample-class distributions, vocabulary sizes, slightly shorter utterance lengths, frequency of the OOS conversations due to multiparty setup, technical issues during the sessions causing unexpected interactions, etc., would all contribute to these shifts. One should also keep in mind the unprecedented group dynamics for that age group in play-based interactions and the unpredictable nature of kids in game-based learning settings. These factors also play some role in the robustness issues of NLU models developed for such challenging real-world deployments.

Besides the inevitable NLU performance degradations on real-world deployment datasets, Table 6 also compares the baseline TF+BERT models with more recent DIET+BERT and DIET+ConveRT architectures, all trained on POC data and tested on in-the-wild game data. The DIET+ConveRT models still reach the highest Intent Recognition F1-scores on these test sets, but the gap between the baseline and the best-performing models has been narrowed, especially for the Watering game. Compared to the TF+BERT baseline, the performance gain with the DIET+ConveRT approach is +3.92% in Planting and only +0.51% in Watering games when tested in-the-wild. For Planting, the increasing performance trends going from TF+BERT to DIET+BERT and DIET+ConveRT are also distinguishable on the deployment set. However, for Watering, the baseline TF+BERT model performs relatively well when tested on the deployment set, achieving only slightly lower F1-scores than the DIET+ConveRT. Notice that the variances are also relatively high in this case, so we may not observe the significant performance benefits when switching to DIET architecture from baseline TF for Watering game deployment. The

Data	Sample Utterance	Intent	Prediction
Planting Game	oh so like green and blue colors?	*answer-valid*	*answer-flowers*
	thirteen flowers!	*counting*	*answer-flowers*
	so if we had to start at a number what number do you think we should start at?	*counting*	*ask-number*
	or twenty less okay so we're going down	*counting*	*out-of-scope*
	let's add let's add a flower pot what do you think?	*counting*	*intro-game*
	yeah totally! do you wanna plant some next to him?	*affirm*	*intro-game*
	yeah I think that's ninety	*affirm*	*counting*
	no I think it was forty five	*deny*	*counting*
	okay so what do we need to start with?	*out-of-scope*	*help-affirm*
Watering Game	next one?	*ask-number*	*next-step*
	okay so how many more do you think we need?	*counting*	*ask-number*
	we need ten more to water	*counting*	*answer-water*
	to give to have enough water to plant our flowers and make them grow	*intro-game*	*answer-water*
	so when we look at these numbers all of the ones with the two in front, have two tens	*intro-game*	*counting*
	if we get four correct answer	*intro-game*	*counting*
	all right he's gotta go get his watering can that he must have put it away	*out-of-scope*	*intro-game*
	the ground	*out-of-scope*	*answer-valid*
	timber what	*out-of-scope*	*answer-valid*

Table 7: NLU/Intent prediction error samples from Planting and Watering games deployed in-the-wild: DIET+ConveRT model trained on KidSpace-PW-POC datasets and tested on KidSpace-PW-Deployment datasets

possible reason for the baseline model in Watering being already quite robust on real-world data could be the size differences in POC datasets on which the models are trained. To be more precise, the Planting baseline model is trained on 1927 samples and tested on 2173 in-the-wild utterances (see Table 3). Unlikely, the Watering baseline model is trained on 2115 samples and tested on 2122 utterances (see Table 4). In addition, we have one less intent class to predict in total (e.g., 14 vs. 13) and two fewer domain-specific intent types (e.g., 10 vs. 8) in the Watering game compared to the Planting. Having around 10% more data for training, plus having slightly less number of total and domain-specific intents, can explain the relatively higher robustness of the baseline model on Watering deployment data (compared to Planting). On the other hand, due to the consistently significant improvements obtained in all other cases (i.e., Planting-POC, Watering-POC, and Planting-Deployment), DIET+ConverRT still seems a promisingly more robust NLU model for our future use-cases.

4.3. Error Analysis and Discussion

In this subsection, we aim to investigate further the differences between the POC and the real-world deployment datasets for NLU in our game-based learning activities. When best-performing DIET+ConveRT models were tested in-the-wild, we discovered overall F1-score performance drops of around 7% for Intent Recognition, consistently for both game activities (i.e., Planting and Watering). When we analyze the intent-wise results, we identify some generalization issues between the POC to in-the-wild datasets, especially with the highly domain-specific intents.

For the Planting Flowers game, the top 5 intent classes with highest performance drops (≥20%) are *answer-valid*, *help-affirm*, *ask-number*, *answer-flowers*, and *intro-game*. Among these, *help-affirm* had quite low test samples (only 4 utterances observed during deployments), which could explain the high variance in the detection performance. Regarding these top 5 erroneous intent classes, we realize that these are highly domain-dependent and activity-specific intent types, where we expect vastly specific answers from the kids based on the game flow design. To illustrate, during this Planting game, kids are helping Oscar to make the meadow look nicer. At the beginning of their interactions, the virtual character is asking *"Let's see, what could we add to the meadow... What kind of plants have pretty colors and smell nice?"* (or something along those lines as we use variations in response templates). We expect the kids to answer with *"flowers"* or its variations at this point in the game, where these short utterances should be classified as *answer-flowers* intent. However, kids can also answer with other plants (or animals, etc.) that belong to the meadow, like *"trees"*, *"bushes"*, *"butterflies"*, *"birds"*, etc. These viable but incorrect answers would ideally be classified as *answer-valid* intent. As you can see, these are extremely task-specific intents, and numerous things can go wrong in-the-wild for these, which may be beyond our assumptions. The *intro-game* intent is also highly game-specific as it is designed to cover the possible utterances from the Facilitator while s/he is introducing the game and explaining the rules (e.g., how to use the big and small pots for 'tens' and 'ones' for this Planting Flowers game). For more generic intent types that can be shared across other activities (e.g., *affirm*, *deny*, *out-of-scope*), we observed relatively less performance degradation in-the-wild using DIET+ConveRT. .

For the Watering game activity, the top 4 intents with highest performance degradations (≥20%) are *answer-valid*, *ask-number*, *intro-game*, and *answer-water*. This time, *answer-valid* had very few test samples (only

6 utterances observed during the Watering game at school sessions), which might again explain the high variance in its performance. All these four intent types are also highly task-specific, and we anticipate more vulnerability for deviations in-the-wild for them, in contrast to the generic intent classes (e.g., *affirm, deny, out-of-scope, goodbye*). During the Watering game, this time, Oscar is asking *"What do you think we need to help the flowers bloom?"*. We expect the kids to answer with *"water"* or its variations, where such utterances should be recognized as *answer-water* intent. Once again, kids can say other viable answers that could help the flowers grow/bloom, such as *"sunlight"*, *"soil"*, *"bees"*, etc., which should be classified as *answer-valid* intent. Similarly, the *intro-game* intent is extremely domain/game-specific and aims to detect Facilitator utterances while s/he is introducing/explaining the game rules (e.g., how to use the number grid projected on the wall for touch-based interactions in this Watering game). Note that these valid answers or game introductions differ substantially based on which game we are playing, and we need to train separate NLU models for each game using these game domain-specific samples.

Table 7 depicts some of the user utterances collected in-the-wild as concrete examples from both deployment datasets. The ground truth intent labels and the predicted intent classes are compared, emphasizing the errors made on some of the most problematic game-specific intents. Here we use our best-performing DIET+ConveRT models for the Intent Classification task. These prediction errors are expected to occur in real-world deployments for various reasons. Some of these user utterances could have multiple intents (e.g., *"yeah totally! do you wanna plant some next to him?"* starts with *affirm*, then the Facilitator continues guiding the kids during *intro-game*). Others could fail due to subtle semantic differences between these classes (e.g., *"if we get four correct answer"* is used by the Facilitator while explaining the NumberGrid game rules but can easily be mixed with *counting* too). There exist some utterances where we see *"flowers"* or *"water"* while *counting* with numbers (e.g., *"thirteen flowers!"*, *"we need ten more to water"*), which are confusing for the models trained on much cleaner datasets. Note that the majority of these classification errors occur for the user utterances during multiparty conversations, i.e., the users are talking to each other instead of Oscar, the virtual game character, but the SDS fails to recognize that (e.g., *"okay so what do we need to start with?"*). These sample utterances also depict several cases where our highly vocal adult Facilitator at school is talking to the kids to introduce the games, explain the rules, guide them to count loudly, and help them find the correct answers in the game flow. It is highly challenging to predict those nearly open-ended conversations and include all possibilities in the POC training datasets to make the NLU models more robust for real-world deployments. However, we are working towards clustering-based semi-supervised intent discovery and human-in-the-loop (HITL) bulk labeling approaches (Sahay et al., 2021; Shen et al., 2021) for cleaner design and separation of intent classes on in-the-wild datasets. We also plan to continue our data augmentation with paraphrase generation efforts to increase the limited POC samples and add more variations during training to make the NLU models more robust in future deployments (Okur et al., 2022).

5. Conclusion

Dialogue systems are vital building blocks to carry out efficient task-oriented communication with children for game play-based learning settings. This study investigates a small step towards improving contextually aware multimodal agents that need to understand and track children's activities and interactions during educational games, support them in performing learning tasks and provide insights to teachers and parents to help personalize the learning experiences. We focus on building task-specific dialogue systems for younger kids learning basic math concepts via gamified interactions. We aim to improve the NLU module of the goal-oriented SDS pipeline with domain-specific game datasets having limited user/player utterances.

In this exploration, we experimented with a flexible and lightweight transformer-based multi-task architecture called DIET (Bunk et al., 2020) to improve the NLU performances on our task-specific game datasets with limited sizes. These domain-specific datasets are manually created for the POC first and then tested on in-the-wild deployment data. Based on the results obtained on POC game datasets, using the DIET classifier with pre-trained ConveRT embeddings has shown to be a promising approach yielding remarkably higher F1-scores for Intent Classification. The NLU results on the real-world deployment game datasets also support these preliminary findings but to a lesser extent.

Using the best performing DIET+ConveRT approach, we observed significant performance drops when the NLU models were tested on in-the-wild game datasets compared to the initial POC datasets. That finding was foreseeable as the player utterances in real-world deployments may usually diverge from the samples within the POC data manually generated for bootstrapping purposes. We investigated these game datasets and shared our exploratory insights for the deviations between POC and in-the-wild datasets. Our preliminary observations suggest that the highest performance shifts occur for the more domain-specific intents in each educational game set. We are working towards making the NLU models and eventually the SDS pipeline more robust for such deviations in-the-wild by empowering the interactive intent labeling with HITL learning techniques and the data augmentation with paraphrasing.

6. Acknowledgements

We thankfully show our gratitude to our current and former colleagues from the Intel Labs Kid Space team, especially Ankur Agrawal, Glen Anderson, Sinem Aslan, Benjamin Bair, Arturo Bringas Garcia, Rebecca Chierichetti, Hector Cordourier Maruri, Pete Denman, Lenitra Durham, Roddy Fuentes Alba, David Gonzalez Aguirre, Sai Prasad, Giuseppe Raffa, Sangita Sharma, and John Sherry, for the conceptualization and the design of use-cases to support this research. In addition, we gratefully acknowledge the Rasa team for the open-source framework and the community developers for their contributions that enabled us to improve our research and build proof-of-concept models for our use-cases.

7. Bibliographical References

Anderson, G. J., Panneer, S., Shi, M., Marshall, C. S., Agrawal, A., Chierichetti, R., Raffa, G., Sherry, J., Loi, D., and Durham, L. M. (2018). Kid space: Interactive learning in a smart environment. In *Proceedings of the Group Interaction Frontiers in Technology*, GIFT'18, New York, NY, USA. Association for Computing Machinery.

Aslan, S., Alyuz, N., Tanriover, C., Mete, S. E., Okur, E., D'Mello, S. K., and Arslan Esme, A. (2019). Investigating the impact of a real-time, multimodal student engagement analytics technology in authentic classrooms. In *Proceedings of the 2019 CHI Conference on Human Factors in Computing Systems*, CHI '19, page 1–12, New York, NY, USA. Association for Computing Machinery.

Aslan, S., Agrawal, A., Alyuz, N., Chierichetti, R., Durham, L. M., Manuvinakurike, R., Okur, E., Sahay, S., Sharma, S., Sherry, J., et al. (2022). Exploring kid space in the wild: a preliminary study of multimodal and immersive collaborative play-based learning experiences. *Educational Technology Research and Development*, pages 1–26.

Bahdanau, D., Cho, K., and Bengio, Y. (2015). Neural machine translation by jointly learning to align and translate. In *International Conference on Learning Representations (ICLR 2015)*.

Baker, R. S. (2021). Artificial intelligence in education: Bringing it all together. *OECD Digital Education Outlook 2021: Pushing the Frontiers with Artificial Intelligence, Blockchain and Robots*, pages 43–51.

Blanchard, N., Brady, M., Olney, A. M., Glaus, M., Sun, X., Nystrand, M., Samei, B., Kelly, S., and D'Mello, S. (2015). A study of automatic speech recognition in noisy classroom environments for automated dialog analysis. In Cristina Conati, et al., editors, *Artificial Intelligence in Education*, pages 23–33, Cham. Springer International Publishing.

Bocklisch, T., Faulkner, J., Pawlowski, N., and Nichol, A. (2017). Rasa: Open source language understanding and dialogue management. In *Conversational AI Workshop, NIPS 2017*.

Bordes, A., Boureau, Y.-L., and Weston, J. (2017). Learning end-to-end goal-oriented dialog. In *International Conference on Learning Representations (ICLR 2017)*.

Bunk, T., Varshneya, D., Vlasov, V., and Nichol, A. (2020). DIET: lightweight language understanding for dialogue systems. *CoRR*, abs/2004.09936.

Burtsev, M., Seliverstov, A., Airapetyan, R., Arkhipov, M., Baymurzina, D., Bushkov, N., Gureenkova, O., Khakhulin, T., Kuratov, Y., Kuznetsov, D., Litinsky, A., Logacheva, V., Lymar, A., Malykh, V., Petrov, M., Polulyakh, V., Pugachev, L., Sorokin, A., Vikhreva, M., and Zaynutdinov, M. (2018). DeepPavlov: Open-source library for dialogue systems. In *Proceedings of ACL 2018, System Demonstrations*, pages 122–127, Melbourne, Australia, July. Association for Computational Linguistics.

Cahill, A., Fife, J. H., Riordan, B., Vajpayee, A., and Galochkin, D. (2020). Context-based automated scoring of complex mathematical responses. In *Proceedings of the Fifteenth Workshop on Innovative Use of NLP for Building Educational Applications*, pages 186–192, Seattle, WA, USA → Online, July. Association for Computational Linguistics.

Chassignol, M., Khoroshavin, A., Klimova, A., and Bilyatdinova, A. (2018). Artificial intelligence trends in education: a narrative overview. *Procedia Computer Science*, 136:16–24. 7th International Young Scientists Conference on Computational Science, YSC2018, 02-06 July2018, Heraklion, Greece.

Cuayáhuitl, H. (2017). Simpleds: A simple deep reinforcement learning dialogue system. In *Dialogues with Social Robots*, pages 109–118. Springer.

Devlin, J., Chang, M.-W., Lee, K., and Toutanova, K. (2019). BERT: Pre-training of deep bidirectional transformers for language understanding. In *Proceedings of the 2019 Conference of the North American Chapter of the Association for Computational Linguistics: Human Language Technologies, Volume 1 (Long and Short Papers)*, pages 4171–4186, Minneapolis, Minnesota, June. Association for Computational Linguistics.

Dhingra, B., Li, L., Li, X., Gao, J., Chen, Y.-N., Ahmed, F., and Deng, L. (2017). Towards end-to-end reinforcement learning of dialogue agents for information access. In *Proceedings of the 55th Annual Meeting of the Association for Computational Linguistics (Volume 1: Long Papers)*, pages 484–495, Vancouver, Canada, July. Association for Computational Linguistics.

Dodge, J., Gane, A., Zhang, X., Bordes, A., Chopra, S., Miller, A. H., Szlam, A., and Weston, J. (2016). Evaluating prerequisite qualities for learning end-to-end dialog systems. In *International Conference on Learning Representations (ICLR 2016)*.

Ghosh, D., Beigman Klebanov, B., and Song, Y.

(2020). An exploratory study of argumentative writing by young students: A transformer-based approach. In *Proceedings of the Fifteenth Workshop on Innovative Use of NLP for Building Educational Applications*, pages 145–150, Seattle, WA, USA → Online, July. Association for Computational Linguistics.

Goo, C.-W., Gao, G., Hsu, Y.-K., Huo, C.-L., Chen, T.-C., Hsu, K.-W., and Chen, Y.-N. (2018). Slot-gated modeling for joint slot filling and intent prediction. In *Proceedings of the 2018 Conference of the North American Chapter of the Association for Computational Linguistics: Human Language Technologies, Volume 2 (Short Papers)*, pages 753–757, New Orleans, Louisiana, June. Association for Computational Linguistics.

Graesser, A. C., Lu, S., Jackson, G. T., Mitchell, H. H., Ventura, M., Olney, A., and Louwerse, M. M. (2004). Autotutor: A tutor with dialogue in natural language. *Behavior Research Methods, Instruments, & Computers*, 36(2):180–192.

Gu, Y., Li, X., Chen, S., Zhang, J., and Marsic, I. (2017). Speech intention classification with multimodal deep learning. In *Canadian conference on artificial intelligence*, pages 260–271. Springer.

Hakkani-Tür, D., Tur, G., Celikyilmaz, A., Chen, Y.-N., Gao, J., Deng, L., and Wang, Y.-Y. (2016). Multi-domain joint semantic frame parsing using bi-directional rnn-lstm. *Interspeech 2016*, pages 715–719.

Henderson, M., Casanueva, I., Mrkšić, N., Su, P.-H., Wen, T.-H., and Vulić, I. (2020). ConveRT: Efficient and accurate conversational representations from transformers. In *Findings of the Association for Computational Linguistics: EMNLP 2020*, pages 2161–2174, Online, November. Association for Computational Linguistics.

Hochreiter, S. and Schmidhuber, J. (1997). Long short-term memory. *Neural computation*, 9(8):1735–1780.

Hooshyar, D., Yousefi, M., and Lim, H. (2019). A systematic review of data-driven approaches in player modeling of educational games. *Artificial Intelligence Review*, 52(3):1997–2017.

Jia, J., He, Y., and Le, H. (2020). A multimodal human-computer interaction system and its application in smart learning environments. In Simon K. S. Cheung, et al., editors, *Blended Learning. Education in a Smart Learning Environment*, pages 3–14, Cham. Springer International Publishing.

Jurafsky, D. and Martin, J. H. (2018). *Ch 24: Dialog Systems and Chatbots. Speech and Language Processing: An Introduction to Natural Language Processing, Computational Linguistics, and Speech Recognition*. Prentice Hall PTR, Upper Saddle River, NJ, USA, 3rd (draft) edition.

Kerry, A., Ellis, R., and Bull, S. (2009). Conversational agents in e-learning. In Tony Allen, et al., editors, *Applications and Innovations in Intelligent Systems XVI*, pages 169–182, London. Springer London.

Lafferty, J. D., McCallum, A., and Pereira, F. C. N. (2001). Conditional random fields: Probabilistic models for segmenting and labeling sequence data. In *International Conference on Machine Learning*, ICML, pages 282–289.

Lende, S. P. and Raghuwanshi, M. (2016). Question answering system on education acts using nlp techniques. In *2016 world conference on futuristic trends in research and innovation for social welfare (Startup Conclave)*, pages 1–6. IEEE.

Lester, J. C., Ha, E. Y., Lee, S. Y., Mott, B. W., Rowe, J. P., and Sabourin, J. L. (2013). Serious games get smart: Intelligent game-based learning environments. *AI Magazine*, 34(4):31–45, Dec.

Litman, D. J. and Silliman, S. (2004). Itspoke: An intelligent tutoring spoken dialogue system. In *Demonstration Papers at HLT-NAACL 2004*, HLT-NAACL–Demonstrations '04, page 5–8, USA. Association for Computational Linguistics.

Liu, B. and Lane, I. (2016). Attention-based recurrent neural network models for joint intent detection and slot filling. In *Interspeech 2016*, pages 685–689.

Liu, B., Tur, G., Hakkani-Tur, D., Shah, P., and Heck, L. (2017). End-to-end optimization of task-oriented dialogue model with deep reinforcement learning. In *Conversational AI Workshop, NIPS 2017*.

Liu, X., Eshghi, A., Swietojanski, P., and Rieser, V., (2021). *Benchmarking Natural Language Understanding Services for Building Conversational Agents*, pages 165–183. Springer Singapore, Singapore.

Mesnil, G., Dauphin, Y., Yao, K., Bengio, Y., Deng, L., Hakkani-Tur, D., He, X., Heck, L., Tur, G., Yu, D., and Zweig, G. (2015). Using recurrent neural networks for slot filling in spoken language understanding. *IEEE/ACM Transactions on Audio, Speech, and Language Processing*, 23(3):530–539, March.

Meurers, D. (2012). Natural language processing and language learning. *Encyclopedia of Applied Linguistics*, pages 4193–4205.

Min, W., Mott, B. W., Rowe, J. P., Liu, B., and Lester, J. C. (2016). Player goal recognition in open-world digital games with long short-term memory networks. In *IJCAI*, pages 2590–2596.

Min, W., Mott, B., Rowe, J., Taylor, R., Wiebe, E., Boyer, K. E., and Lester, J. (2017). Multimodal goal recognition in open-world digital games. In *Proceedings of the Thirteenth AAAI Conference on Artificial Intelligence And Interactive Digital Entertainment*, volume 13, pages 80–86.

Okur, E., Kumar, S. H., Sahay, S., Esme, A. A., and Nachman, L. (2019). Natural language interactions in autonomous vehicles: Intent detection and slot filling from passenger utterances. *20th International*

Conference on Computational Linguistics and Intelligent Text Processing (CICLing 2019), April.

Okur, E., H Kumar, S., Sahay, S., and Nachman, L. (2020). Audio-visual understanding of passenger intents for in-cabin conversational agents. In *Second Grand-Challenge and Workshop on Multimodal Language (Challenge-HML), ACL 2020*, pages 55–59, Seattle, USA, July. Association for Computational Linguistics.

Okur, E., Sahay, S., and Nachman, L. (2022). Data augmentation with paraphrase generation and entity extraction for multimodal dialogue system. In *Proceedings of the 13th International Conference on Language Resources and Evaluation (LREC 2022)*.

Palasundram, K., Sharef, N. M., Nasharuddin, N., Kasmiran, K., and Azman, A. (2019). Sequence to sequence model performance for education chatbot. *International Journal of Emerging Technologies in Learning (iJET)*, 14(24):56–68, December.

Pennington, J., Socher, R., and Manning, C. (2014). GloVe: Global vectors for word representation. In *Proceedings of the 2014 Conference on Empirical Methods in Natural Language Processing (EMNLP)*, pages 1532–1543, Doha, Qatar, October. Association for Computational Linguistics.

Pires, A. C., González Perilli, F., Bakała, E., Fleisher, B., Sansone, G., and Marichal, S. (2019). Building blocks of mathematical learning: Virtual and tangible manipulatives lead to different strategies in number composition. *Frontiers in Education*, 4.

Raamadhurai, S., Baker, R., and Poduval, V. (2019). Curio SmartChat : A system for natural language question answering for self-paced k-12 learning. In *Proceedings of the Fourteenth Workshop on Innovative Use of NLP for Building Educational Applications*, pages 336–342, Florence, Italy, August. Association for Computational Linguistics.

Richey, J. E., Zhang, J., Das, R., Andres-Bray, J. M., Scruggs, R., Mogessie, M., Baker, R. S., and McLaren, B. M. (2021). Gaming and confrustion explain learning advantages for a math digital learning game. In Ido Roll, et al., editors, *Artificial Intelligence in Education*, pages 342–355, Cham. Springer International Publishing.

Roos, S. (2018). Chatbots in education: A passing trend or a valuable pedagogical tool? Master's thesis, Uppsala University, Department of Informatics and Media.

Sahay, S., Kumar, S. H., Okur, E., Syed, H., and Nachman, L. (2019). Modeling intent, dialog policies and response adaptation for goal-oriented interactions. In *Proceedings of the 23rd Workshop on the Semantics and Pragmatics of Dialogue*, London, United Kingdom, September. SEMDIAL.

Sahay, S., Okur, E., Hakim, N., and Nachman, L. (2021). Semi-supervised interactive intent labeling. In *Proceedings of the Second Workshop on Data Science with Human in the Loop: Language Advances, NAACL 2021*, pages 31–40, Online, June. Association for Computational Linguistics.

Schuster, M. and Paliwal, K. K. (1997). Bidirectional recurrent neural networks. *IEEE Transactions on Signal Processing*, 45(11):2673–2681, November.

Shah, P., Hakkani-Tur, D., and Heck, L. (2016). Interactive reinforcement learning for task-oriented dialogue management. In *Deep Learning for Action and Interaction Workshop, NIPS 2016*.

Shen, X., Sun, Y., Zhang, Y., and Najmabadi, M. (2021). Semi-supervised intent discovery with contrastive learning. In *Proceedings of the 3rd Workshop on Natural Language Processing for Conversational AI*, pages 120–129, Online, November. Association for Computational Linguistics.

Skene, K., O'Farrelly, C. M., Byrne, E. M., Kirby, N., Stevens, E. C., and Ramchandani, P. G. (2022). Can guidance during play enhance children's learning and development in educational contexts? a systematic review and meta-analysis. *Child Development*.

Su, P.-H., Budzianowski, P., Ultes, S., Gasic, M., and Young, S. (2017). Sample-efficient actor-critic reinforcement learning with supervised data for dialogue management. In *Proceedings of the 18th Annual SIGdial Meeting on Discourse and Dialogue*, pages 147–157, Saarbrücken, Germany, August. Association for Computational Linguistics.

Sun, Y., Play, T., Nambiar, R., and Vidyasagaran, V. (2021). Gamifying math education using object detection. In *Workshop on Math AI for Education (MATHAI4ED), 35th Conference on Neural Information Processing Systems (NeurIPS 2021)*.

Taghipour, K. and Ng, H. T. (2016). A neural approach to automated essay scoring. In *Proceedings of the 2016 Conference on Empirical Methods in Natural Language Processing*, pages 1882–1891, Austin, Texas, November. Association for Computational Linguistics.

Ultes, S., Rojas Barahona, L. M., Su, P.-H., Vandyke, D., Kim, D., Casanueva, I., Budzianowski, P., Mrkšić, N., Wen, T.-H., Gasic, M., and Young, S. (2017). PyDial: A multi-domain statistical dialogue system toolkit. In *Proceedings of ACL 2017, System Demonstrations*, pages 73–78, Vancouver, Canada, July. Association for Computational Linguistics.

Vanzo, A., Bastianelli, E., and Lemon, O. (2019). Hierarchical multi-task natural language understanding for cross-domain conversational AI: HERMIT NLU. In *Proceedings of the 20th Annual SIGdial Meeting on Discourse and Dialogue*, pages 254–263, Stockholm, Sweden, September. Association for Computational Linguistics.

Varghese, A. S., Sarang, S., Yadav, V., Karotra, B., and Gandhi, N. (2020). Bidirectional lstm joint model for intent classification and named entity recognition in natural language understanding. *International Journal of Hybrid Intelligent Systems*, 16(1):13–23.

Vaswani, A., Shazeer, N., Parmar, N., Uszkoreit, J., Jones, L., Gomez, A. N., Kaiser, L., and Polosukhin, I. (2017). Attention is all you need. In *Advances in Neural Information Processing Systems 30: Annual Conference on Neural Information Processing Systems 2017, 4-9 December 2017, Long Beach, CA, USA*, pages 5998–6008.

Wen, L., Wang, X., Dong, Z., and Chen, H. (2018). Jointly modeling intent identification and slot filling with contextual and hierarchical information. In Xuanjing Huang, et al., editors, *Natural Language Processing and Chinese Computing*, pages 3–15, Cham. Springer International Publishing.

Winkler, R. and Söllner, M. (2018). Unleashing the potential of chatbots in education: A state-of-the-art analysis. In *Academy of Management Annual Meeting (AOM)*.

Winkler, R., Hobert, S., Salovaara, A., Söllner, M., and Leimeister, J. M., (2020). *Sara, the Lecturer: Improving Learning in Online Education with a Scaffolding-Based Conversational Agent*, page 1–14. Association for Computing Machinery, New York, NY, USA.

Wu, L., Fisch, A., Chopra, S., Adams, K., Bordes, A., and Weston, J. (2018). Starspace: Embed all the things! In *Proceedings of the Thirty-Second AAAI Conference on Artificial Intelligence*, volume 32.

Zhai, X., Chu, X., Chai, C. S., Jong, M. S. Y., Istenic, A., Spector, M., Liu, J.-B., Yuan, J., and Li, Y. (2021). A review of artificial intelligence (AI) in education from 2010 to 2020. *Complexity*, 2021.

Zhang, K. and Aslan, A. B. (2021). AI technologies for education: Recent research & future directions. *Computers and Education: Artificial Intelligence*, 2:100025.

Zhang, X. and Wang, H. (2016). A joint model of intent determination and slot filling for spoken language understanding. In *Proceedings of the Twenty-Fifth International Joint Conference on Artificial Intelligence*, IJCAI'16, pages 2993–2999. AAAI Press.

Zhou, Q., Wen, L., Wang, X., Ma, L., and Wang, Y. (2016). A hierarchical lstm model for joint tasks. In Maosong Sun, et al., editors, *Chinese Computational Linguistics and Natural Language Processing Based on Naturally Annotated Big Data*, pages 324–335, Cham. Springer International Publishing.

Proceedings of the 9th Games and Natural Language Processing Workshop @LREC2022, pages 40–48
Marseille, 25 June 2022

How NLP Can Strengthen Digital Game-Based Language Learning Resources for Less Resourced Languages

Monica Ward[1], Liang Xu[1], Elaine Uí Dhonnchadha[2]
[1] Dublin City University, Ireland
[2] Trinity College Dublin, Ireland
monica.ward@dcu.ie, liang.xu6@mail.dcu.ie, uidhonne@tcd.ie

Abstract

This paper provides an overview of the Cipher engine which enables the development of a Digital Educational Game (DEG) based on noticing ciphers or patterns in texts. The Cipher engine was used to develop the *Cipher: Faoi Gheasa*, a digital educational game for Irish, which incorporates NLP resources and is informed by Digital Game-Based Language Learning (DGBLL) and Computer-Assisted Language Learning (CALL) research. The paper outlines six phases where NLP has strengthened the *Cipher: Faoi Gheasa* game. It shows how the Cipher engine can be used to build a Cipher game for other languages, particularly low-resourced and endangered languages in which NLP resources are under-developed or few in number.

Keywords: Digital educational game, digital game-based language learning, low-resourced language, computer-assisted language learning

1. Introduction

NLP technologies are designed to interact with human language for a variety of purposes including speech recognition, natural language understanding and natural language generation. Digital Educational Games (DEG) involve the use of computer game characteristics for educational purposes with a focus on learner engagement. NLP technologies can be used in games to improve the experience for players, especially for Digital Game-Based Language Learning (DGBLL) in which learning languages is a desired side effect of playing games. Computer-Assisted Language Learning (CALL) involves the use of technology in the language learning process. It encompasses DGBLL but is broader in reach as it also covers other approaches to language learning. CALL resources can be used in traditional learning settings as well as online, offline and in individual learning spaces. In the paper, we discuss how players can be encouraged to notice errors (ciphers) in texts and in a game. This allows them to become aware of errors in Irish spelling and grammar which is something they often do not notice or are unaware of. This game can provide valuable learning opportunities for language learners including vocabulary, reading and writing practice. Section 2 provides an overview of the role of motivation in language learning and particularly the issue of reluctant learners of Irish. It looks at Digital Game-Based Language Learning and NLP-infused games in CALL. Section 3 describes the methodology and gives a brief explanation of the Cipher engine and the six phases in the Cipher pipeline with an NLP component. Section 4 outlines the implementation of the game, while Section 5 provides the results and evaluation of the game. Section 6 covers the discussion and section 7 is future work. Section 8 gives the overall conclusion of the paper.

2. Background and Related Work

2.1 Motivation

Language learning can be interesting, stimulating and fun. However, for many learners who have to learn a language it can be uncomfortable, boring and not enjoyable. Many second language (L2) learners are reluctant learners particularly when it is a compulsory subject in their education system. Some of the world's L2 English learners fall into this category. There are several challenges for these reluctant learners. Protheroe (2004) notes that they do not complete tasks and they avoid challenges, even though they are capable of excelling. Sanacore (2007) highlights the importance of fostering intrinsic motivation with reluctant learners. He makes four suggestions to help reluctant learners. He states that it is important to create a learning environment that is encouraging and challenging. Sometimes teachers think they have to simplify things to the point at which there is no challenge for the student, but even beginning language learners should have opportunities to engage in challenging learning activities. Students should be provided with opportunities to make learning choices. Student choice brings many positive benefits including increasing their autonomous behaviour, eliciting cognitive flexibility, high task interest, positive emotion, creativity, and persistence (Clifford 2007; Deci and Ryan 1987). Sometimes students are passive learners in their lessons and Sanacore (2007) advocates for increasing students' participation in classroom activities as a way to foster intrinsic motivation. The aim of a teacher should be to encourage students to love learning as this will make learning activities more enjoyable and fruitful for students.

Although Irish is one of the three official languages of Ireland (English and Irish Sign Language are the other two), it is only spoken by 1.5% of the population outside of the education system on a daily basis (CSO, 2016). With some exceptions, it is a compulsory subject in both primary and post-primary schools. Students often lack motivation to study the language and this can make Irish lessons seem like drudgery rather than an enjoyable experience for some students. The teachers, who in the majority of cases are not native speakers, often have to shoulder the burden of Irish language education as many parents are not able to help their children with their Irish homework. Until recently, there were very few interactive resources for teaching Irish in the school context. There are now some online resources linked to specific textbooks, but these are limited in number. Irish is not considered as a Modern Foreign Language (MFL) in the Irish school system which means that some of the pedagogical innovations from the MFL field do not find their way into the teaching of Irish. This is unfortunate, as many of these innovations can help to make the learning experience more engaging and personalised for the students (e.g., Ward et al., 2019). In a recent report, Irish language inspectors noted the need for enhanced Irish language learning activities.

> "*Inspectors observed an overreliance on translation from Irish to English as part of the pupils' experience of Irish and highlighted a need for more fun and engaging Irish language learning activities.*" - The Irish Times (23/03/2022)

In the Irish context, just as Sanacore (2007) outlined for reluctant learners in general, there is a need to provide challenging learning activities, offer student choice and provide opportunities for more active learning. One way of providing these activities and opportunities is with the use of a Digital Game-Based Language Learning (DGBLL) app for Irish.

2.2 Digital Game-Based Language Learning

Sørensen and Meyer (2007) discussed the trend of technology in language learning moving away from rote-based acquisition that focuses on drills, grammatical structures and translation tests to context-based acquisition that focuses on task-based, project-based and content-based approaches. Games can be seen as a lever for the transformation. In fact, game progression depends on players' performance of skills which are based on their actions in games rather than simply memorising information or giving correct answers (Dunkel, 1991). Performance is expected in game-based activities while schools tend to focus on tests and competence (Gee, 2005). For instance, people may be more willing to read game-related text (e.g., in-game text, game walkthrough, supplementary materials) in order to win a game instead of reading a linear text assigned to them for a test and in this way their comprehension would increase with each repetition (Underwood, 1987).

The idea of digital game-based learning (DGBLL) has proven to be supportive for L2 learning. In recent years, an increasing number of studies have analysed the impact of digital games on L2 developments and these studies have led to several meta-analysis studies. Findings from these studies have reached the conclusion that digital games have positive effects on L2 learning, particularly on L2 vocabulary (Dixon et al., 2022; Chen et al., 2018; Tsai and Tsai, 2018). Dixon et al., (2022) suggested that DGBLL works better for games designed for entertainment than games designed for educational purposes and that the latter has been overlooked by the CALL community. This is mainly due to the fact that DEGs lack commercial interest from industry and the too "obvious" objectives of language learning further limits a DEG's success (Reinhardt, 2019). Moreover, DEGs are often overshadowed by games designed for entertainment when it comes to engaging elements (e.g., storylines) and authentic language interaction (e.g., spoken and written input) (Dixon et al., 2022).

However, DEGs have the advantage of providing learners with access to minority languages. The language options of games designed for entertainment are very limited and are mainly available for 'bigger' languages e.g., English and Spanish. For games designed for entertainment, the incentive for adding other languages would be much lower compared to DEGs or entertainment apps specifically designed for language learning purposes. For example, there are more than 40 different languages in Duolingo including many minority languages according to the 2021 Duolingo language report (Blanco, 2021) and the number has been increasing. Therefore, DEGs can be important for supporting the learning and teaching of minority languages.

2.3 NLP Infused Games and CALL

NLP resources have the potential to contribute to Computer-Assisted Language Learning (CALL) (Ward, 2019), but this potential remains largely under-utilised. While some NLP resources have been used in CALL to date, this is often as a by-product of NLP research rather than an explicitly stated aim of the NLP resources. A basic impediment to the use of NLP resources in CALL is that there is limited overlap and interaction between the NLP and CALL communities in general. NLP researchers focus mainly on language and linguistic technologies (with limited consideration for pedagogy) while CALL researchers prefer to focus on pedagogy first and technology second.

There are many reasons for the limited use of NLP resources in CALL, but the two overarching ones are that the development of CALL resources is challenging (Godwin-Jones, 2015) and the overall difficulty of incorporating NLP technologies into CALL resources (Heift & Schulze, 2007). Ideally, the development of CALL resources would involve a range of experts including language teachers, linguists, pedagogical designers, software engineers, user interface (UI) designers and educational technologists amongst others. It is rare for CALL teams to have access to this range of experts, particularly given the limited time and financial resources available to most CALL development teams. The development of NLP resources is also challenging and most NLP resources are designed to deal with native or near-native speakers rather than foreign language learners. The errors that are inherent in language produced by learners can be very challenging for NLP resources that expect native-like language input. Language learning involves five main language skills (reading, writing, listening, speaking and interacting) and NLP has the potential to contribute to CALL in all of these areas (Ward, 2017; Ward, 2019). Many language learners currently use NLP-embedded tools for writing (e.g., spelling and grammar checkers (Ferris et al., 2013)) and text-to-speech tools can also be helpful to learners (e.g., Cardoso et al., 2015), especially if they are unfamiliar with the L2 writing system.

3. Methodology

3.1 Cipher Engine

CALL research is heavily focussed on the most commonly taught languages, particularly English. This is not surprising as there are around 1.5 billion English language learners in the world (British Council, 2014). This means that most of the CALL resources developed are for learners of English and to a lesser extent Spanish, French and German. Consequently, there are fewer resources for Less Commonly Taught Languages (LCTLs) (Ward, 2015), which can range from languages with a large number of speakers such as Chinese and Arabic to languages widely spoken in their country of origin such as Polish and Thai. The term LCTL also covers minority or regional languages like Catalan and endangered languages like North Saami (see Ward, 2018 for more details). A language can be an official language of a country and yet be a Less Commonly Taught language. This is the case for Irish. Notwithstanding the large Irish diaspora, on a worldwide scale there are very few learners of Irish. It is more challenging to develop CALL resources for LCTLs (Ward, 2015) and therefore LCLT CALL researchers sometimes are creative (e.g., Millour et al., 2020) or aim to leverage existing resources and adapt them to their own LCTL (e.g., Purgina et al., 2017).

This is the case in the development of *Cipher: Faoi Gheasa*, which was based on the original Cipher game (Xu and Chamberlain, 2020) for advanced level English language users (B1 - C2, on the Council of Europe CEFR scale). Cipher is a crowdsourcing game designed for identifying errors in text which uses the idea of 'games with a purpose' (GWAP) (Von Ahn, 2006). Error spotting was gamified such that people were encouraged to spot errors in texts through the game. While playing the game, players are making annotations to the text, and thus data is collected for further analysis. The results showed that people could easily notice text errors in the game and it is therefore possible to identify errors using a game. Moreover, feedback from users indicated that Cipher was fun to play and has potential to help language learning.

Cipher: Faoi Gheasa was adapted to cater for Irish language learners of A2-B1 level. A new storyline, new game features and elements, and updated rules were added to the original Cipher engine to encourage language learning and facilitate in-game data collection. The theme of "reconnecting to the spirit of the language" (Napier & Whiskeyjack, 2021) functions as the socio-cultural background behind the game design.

3.2 A Language Independent Cipher Engine

It can be more challenging to develop DGBLL resources for Less Commonly Taught Languages (LCTLs) and therefore where possible, DGBLL developers should aim to develop resources that are language independent. In other words, the framework should be decoupled from the language so that a plug and play approach can be used. With this approach, language specific modules can be added to the template to create a DGBL resource for that specific language. While pedagogical issues may arise due to the range of human languages, where possible a language independent approach is beneficial for the development of DGBLL resources for LCTLs and this is the approach adopted in the design and development of the Cipher engine.

3.3 Game Mechanics

We focus on three language tasks in this game: noticing, reading, and writing. Integrated with interesting game elements, these language tasks are mapped onto game tasks which fit into the game storyline and the theme of "reconnecting to the spirit of the language". The storyline is as follows:

1. There is an **evil game character** whose goal is to make ancient tales unreadable to people by casting spells upon the tales in which many ancient mythological creatures dwell. The evil spirit, Syfer, wishes to make people forget the tales and ensure that these mythical beings will eventually vanish as their existence is based on people's belief in them. The aim of the player is to defeat the evil Syfer.
2. The players need to **read stories** and **find the enchanted words** and **identify the spells** that were cast upon the words.
3. The design of the spells is inspired by the idea of **steganography** following the original Cipher game (Xu and Chamberlain, 2020). A spell changes certain words (these modified words are known as enchanted words in the game) in the story in a particular way so that the players can identify a spell by finding patterns of errors in the story. This can help the practice of spelling and reading. For ease of understanding, we also refer to spells as ciphers in this paper.
4. Some spells (ciphers) are associated with the **grammatical information** (e.g., word gender), which is designed to help learners get to know more about the vocabulary.
5. If the players fail to find a spell, they will be asked to change the ending of the story in order to delay forgetting of the story and of the magical beings involved. This is designed to help the practice of **writing**.

In addition, there are *power-ups* available for the players to use in case they get stuck. Besides adding more fun to the game, the design of power-ups enables players with little or no knowledge of the language to still be able to enjoy the game. In summary, the task of the player in the game is to find the enchanted words and identify spells cast by Syfer (the evil game character) and thereby save the ancient spirits and the stories. The incentive of the game is to gain spirit power which is a token in the game. Players will gain tokens if they do the "right things" in the game, which includes finding errors, finding ciphers and continuing the story. Players' tokens will be deducted by clicking a word that is not an error, clicking a cipher that is not "responsible" for the errors, using power-ups or abandoning a story.

Cipher: Faoi Gheasa adapts to the player's language level. If a text is too easy for a player, they are shown a more difficult text the next time. Conversely, if a text is too difficult for a player, they are shown an easier text the next time. Furthermore, the difficulties of ciphers are adaptive. The choice of ciphers used in the game text is reflected by players' performance. Figure 1 shows the logic of the adaptability of *Cipher: Faoi Gheasa.*

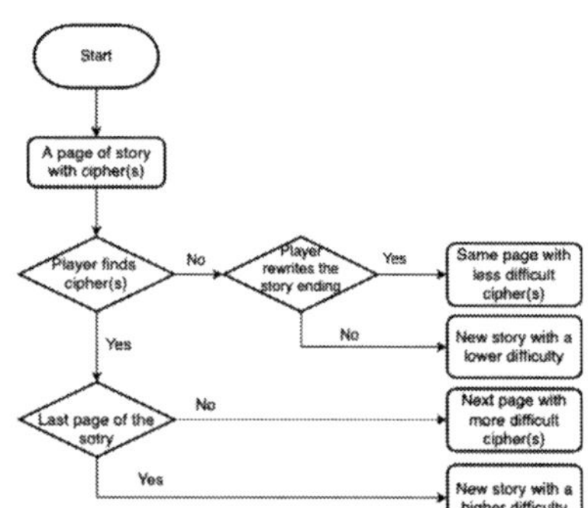

Figure 1: Adaptivity in *Cipher: Faoi Gheasa* using level analyser

4. Implementation

NLP resources and tools have contributed in different ways to the development of *Cipher: Faoi Gheasa*. For example, POS tagging is used for text level analysis, cipher detection analysis, and the analysis of player written texts in learner corpus collection.

4.1 Pre-Processing

It is important to ensure that the texts presented to the players have no spelling or grammatical errors (apart from those introduced by the Cipher engine). There are currently three main sources of texts for *Cipher: Faoi Gheasa*: Dúchas[1] texts, original texts based on traditional Irish stories and international fairy tales and a limited number of texts from the Gutenberg Project[2]. The selected Dúchas texts were stories written by children in the 1940s. These texts were not written in the Official Standard for Irish (*An Caighdeán Oifigiúil*[3]) and needed to be converted to the modern standard. NLP tools were used to detect spelling combinations that needed to be updated. In addition, some of the older texts used the Gaelic font, for example, ċ needed to be replaced by ch. Once these changes had been made, all the texts were reviewed for errors using the online the electronic version of *Ó Dónaill's Irish-English Dictionary*[4] and *Gramadóir*[5] spelling and grammar checker for Irish. Figure 2 shows this preprocessing step.

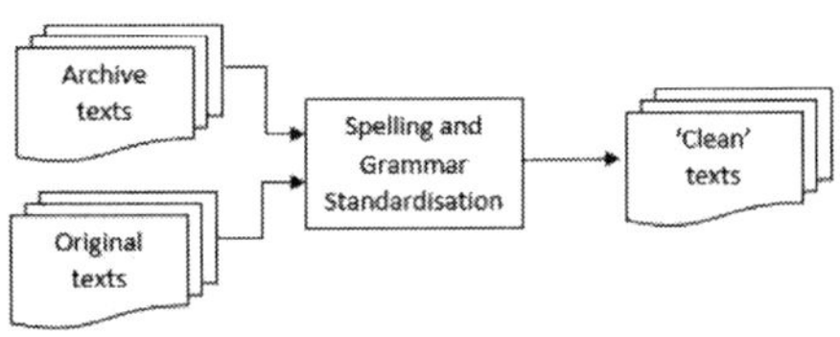

Figure 2: Pre-Processing step

4.2 POS tagging

A POS tagger for Irish (Uí Dhonnchadha and van Genabith, 2006) provides XML formatted POS tagged text to the Cipher engine so it can choose to highlight particular parts of speech. The tagger which was initially developed for general Irish texts, can provide useful information for educational purposes as well. Figure 3 shows the POS-tagging step.

Noun gender is important when learning Irish vocabulary, but it is rarely taught explicitly in schools and students are often unaware of the concept of gender in Irish. Most of the Irish language learners in Ireland are L1 English speakers and they are unfamiliar with the concept of grammatical gender. In *Cipher: Faoi Gheasa*, we draw attention to the gender of nouns by highlighting masculine and feminine nouns in different colours.

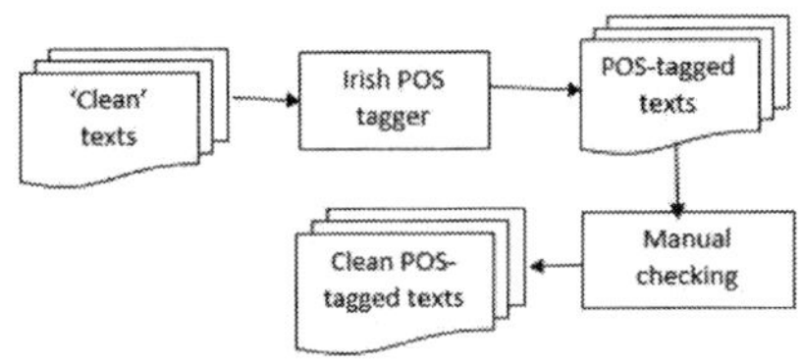

Figure 3: POS-tagging step

Figure 4 shows an example where the word *dullahan* 'dark man', a masculine noun is highlighted in sapphire blue (representing the colour of the Water Spirit) and the word *murúch* 'mermaid', a feminine noun is highlighted in ruby red (representing the colour of the Fire Spirit). Figure 4 explains gender highlighting in the context of the game in a way that fits into the game storyline.

Figure 4: Game storyline explanation of noun gender highlighting

Figure 5 shows a page of a story where all masculine nouns (e.g., *lá* 'day' and *ocras* 'hunger') are coloured blue while the feminine nouns (*tine*, 'fire' and *cailleach* 'witch') are coloured red.

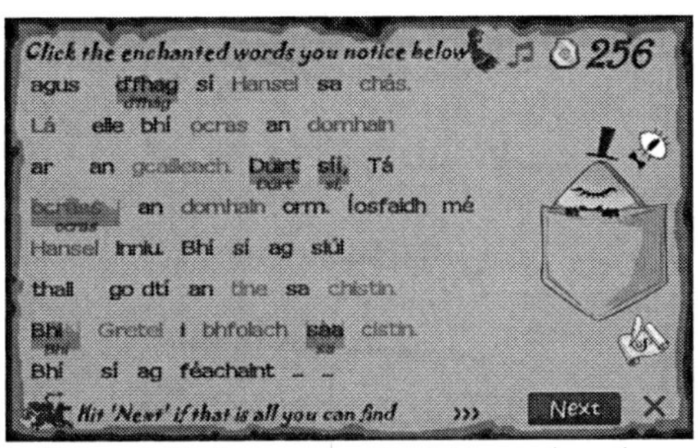

Figure 5: Cipher screen with ciphers and gender highlighted

The names Hansel and Gretel are also coloured according to their gender but words tagged as proper nouns by the POS tagger are excluded from ciphers as there is variability in the ways in which names are spelled and it can be difficult to determine whether a cipher has been applied or not. For illustration purposes the ciphers and their correct forms are shown in Figure 5.

[1] https://www.duchas.ie/en/meitheal/
[2] https://www.gutenberg.org/browse/languages/ga
[3] https://data.oireachtas.ie/ie/oireachtas/caighdeanOifigiul/2017/2017-08-03_an-caighdean-oifigiuil-2017_en.pdf
[4] https://www.teanglann.ie/en/fgb/
[5] https://cadhan.com/gramadoir/foirm-en.html

Normally, when a player is playing the game, the correct forms are not shown (see Figure 6) unless power-ups (see Figure 7) are used.

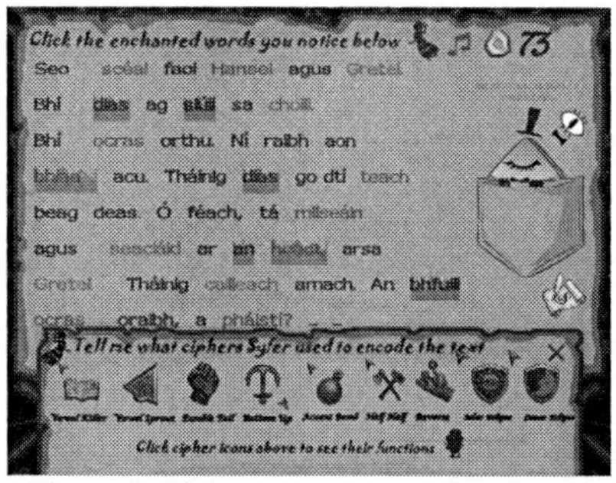

Figure 6: Cipher screen as seen by players

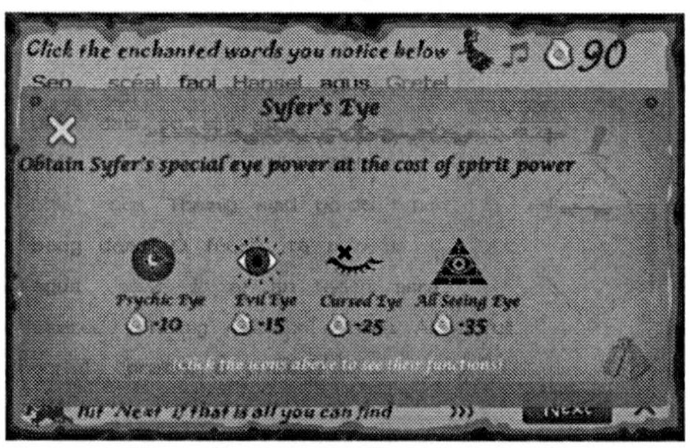

Figure 7: A screenshot of power-ups

There is also a version of *Cipher: Faoi Gheasa* with an Irish language interface but the English language version is shown here for illustration purposes. The Cipher engine can be easily reconfigured to focus on different aspects of language as desired e.g., noun plurals or particular verb tenses.

4.3 Text level analyser

Vygotsky's (1978) Zone of Proximal Development (ZPD) is an important concept in learning in general and is very relevant in language learning contexts. In the Cipher game, it is important that learners are presented with texts at the appropriate level for their language ability. If a text is too hard, the learners will be demotivated and will not want to play the game. If it is too easy, they will be disinterested. A text that has a level of linguistic difficulty that is suitable for the learner will be most engaging for them and will incentivise them to play the game. A combination of NLP tools provides information that can be used to determine the linguistic complexity of a piece of text. There are several checkers available for this in English e.g., Flesch–Kincaid readability tests (Kincaid et al, 1975). There are currently no publicly available text analysis tools for Irish, however the Irish NLP tools[6] are used to provide information about lexical and grammatical complexity which is used to rank the Irish texts used in *Cipher: Faoi Gheasa*. Figure 8 shows the steps in the lexical analysis process.

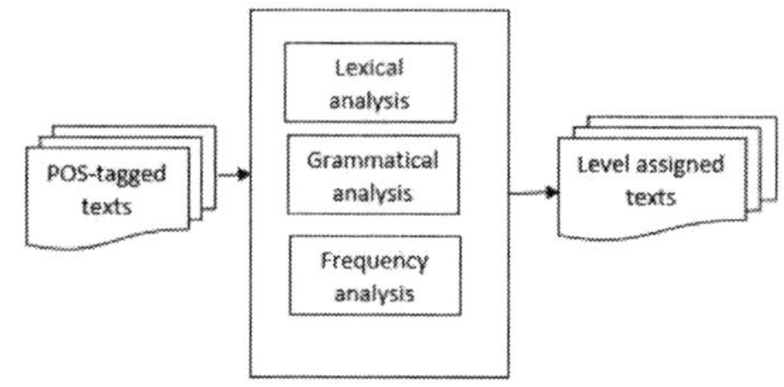

Figure 8: Level analysis phase

4.4 Analysis of Player Cipher Detection

Once the players have played *Cipher: Faoi Gheasa*, their game metrics are stored for analysis. It is helpful to use the Irish POS tagger to classify this data to get better insights into the level of knowledge and awareness that the players have of Irish spelling. Figure 9 shows the steps in the analysis of the cipher detection phase. There are three specific metrics that are calculated:

1. Ciphers correctly identified by players (true positives)
2. Ciphers missed by players (false negatives)
3. Ciphers incorrectly identified by players (false positives)

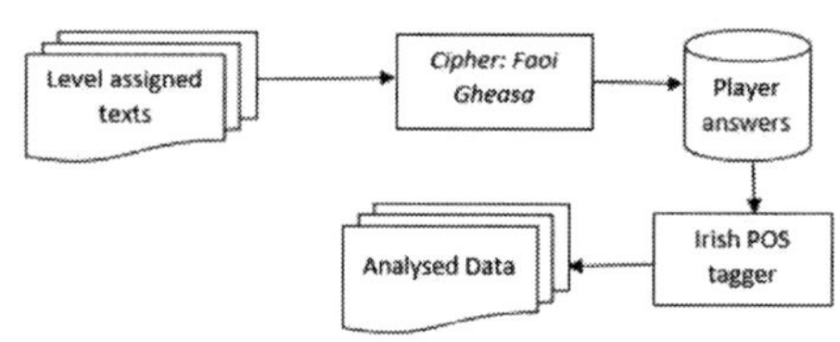

Figure 9: Analysis of cipher detection phase

4.5 Analysis of Player Texts

If players fail to identify a sufficient number of ciphers in a page of text, they have the option of entering a sentence to change the ending of the story. The sentences entered in this way can be analysed to provide further insight into the players' understanding of the text they have read and to give some insight into their level of Irish. The Irish POS tagger can detect if the text is correct Irish (with POS information), incorrect Irish or English (see Section 5.4 for details). Figure 10 shows the analysis phase of players' texts.

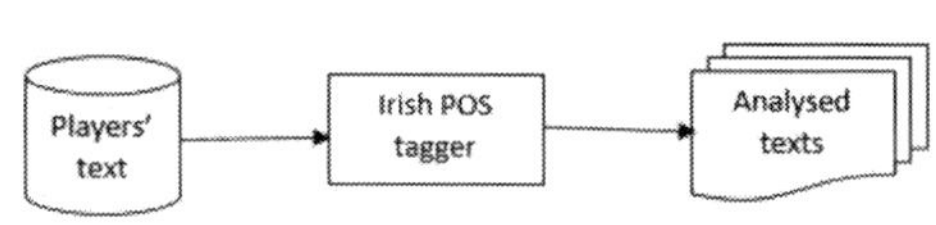

Figure 10: Analysis of players' texts

4.6 Learner Corpus Collection

The sentences entered by the players can be collated to form a corpus of learner Irish. Currently, there is no such publicly available learner corpus from a game for Irish. The

6 https://www.scss.tcd.ie/~uidhonne/irish.utf8.htm

use of *Cipher: Faoi Gheasa* will enable the development of such a corpus.

4.7 NLP Pipeline

The NLP pipeline can help to build other versions of Cipher that are language-specific and culture-specific. The game will work the same way but can be customised for different languages. Figure 11 provides an overview of the NLP pipeline for *Cipher: Faoi Gheasa*. It shows the role of each NLP component in the creation of *Cipher: Faoi Gheasa* and the subsequent analysis of the players' actions while playing the game.

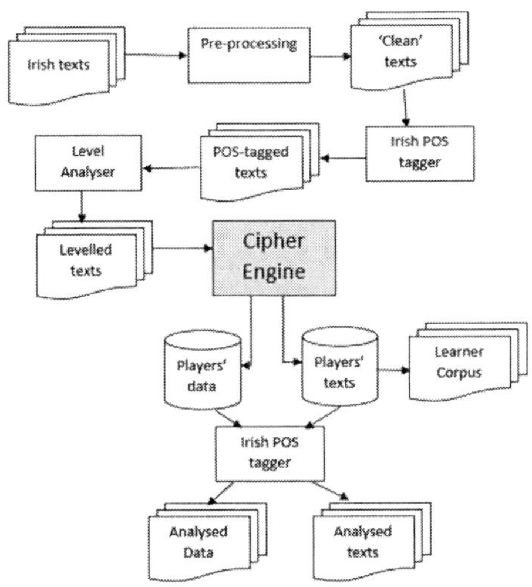

Figure 11: NLP pipeline for Cipher: Faoi: Gheasa

4.8 Choice of materials

We chose the theme of stories and myths for this game as we wish to engage the learners and hold their attention. By choosing familiar fairy tales at the lower levels we can build the learner's knowledge from their L1. At the more advanced levels we use folk tales and mythology which are engaging and can be made culture-specific and reflects the theme of "reconnecting to the spirit of the language". Currently we are using stories from two online archives: www.Dúchas.ie and www.Gutenberg.org, as well as some Irish versions of well-known fairy tales.

5. Results and Evaluation

5.1 POS tagging

The Cipher engine was able to use the XML-formatted POS tagged texts directly and could generate the relevant highlighting features without difficulty.

5.2 Text Level Analyser

This information was useful in deciding which texts to show players. It was particularly helpful for the beginner level as sometimes it can be difficult to realise how limited beginner level students' language knowledge actually is. It can be tempting to add elaborate texts to the game, but if they are beyond the player's Zone of Proximal Development, then they will be off-putting for students. One student commented that "the level of irish was about right but a few verbs that we didn't learn yet". In a pilot study in one primary school where nine classes of 10–12-year-olds tried out the game, approximately 47% of students who filled out a questionnaire think the difficulty level of the game text is about right. (Figure 12)

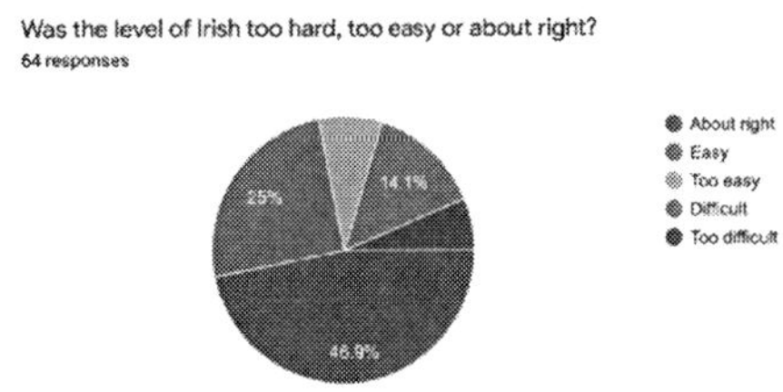

Figure 12: Students' opinions of the difficulty of the game text

5.3 Analysis of student cipher detection

5.3.1 Ciphers correctly identified by players

The POS tagger was useful in classifying the information on cipher detection by the players. In the case of occurrences of an error (where it was seen more than 20 times), there is a mix of POS categories in the correctly identified errors. Most of these words would be familiar to players (e.g., *choill* 'wood', *bhia* 'food' and *mhuc* 'pig'), while the ciphered words are unlikely *(scrao, uca) or* impossible in Irish (*hcaet, htiam*). Table 1 shows the top 10 ciphered words correctly identified by players.

Ciphered Word	Correct word	Lemma	Meaning	POS
lhoilc	choill	coill	forest	N(m)
scrao	ocras	ocras	hunger	N(m)
uca	acu	ag	at	Prep.
hcaet	teach	teach	house	N(m)
arsaa	arsa	arsa	said	V(past)
bhíí	bhí	bí	was	V(past)
niáeslim	milseán	milseán	sweet	N(m)
gaeb	beag	beag	small	Adj.
htiam	maith	maith	good	Adj.
hraibo	oraibh	ar	on you (pl)	Prep. Pron.

Table 1: Ciphers correctly identified by players

5.3.2 Ciphers Not Identified

There is also a mix of POS categories where the ciphers were not identified by the players. It is interesting to note that the words (*ocras* 'hunger' and *siad* 'said') are repeated in the lists, with different ciphers. Table 2 shows the top 6 ciphers missed by players.

Ciphered Word	Correct word	Lemma	Meaning	POS
ann	an	an	the	Art(d)
asra	arsa	arsa	said	V(past)
dias	siad	siad	them	Pro(3P)
dais	siad	siad	them	Pro(3P)
sarco	ocras	ocras	hunger	N(m)
nna	ann	ann	there	Adv.

Table 2: Ciphers not identified by players

5.3.3 Ciphers Identified Incorrectly

Table 3 shows the top 10 words incorrectly identified by players as ciphers, when they were in fact correctly spelt. The word most often incorrectly identified as an incorrect spelling was *arsa* 'said'. While this is commonly used in stories to indicate direct speech, it may not have featured very often in the students' textbooks. It is interesting to note that nouns (*choill, bhia, lapadaíl*) were frequently incorrectly identified as being ciphers, followed by adverbs (*anall, anonn*). Both *choill* and *bhia* have initial mutations and students may be more familiar with the unmutated lemma forms *coill* and *bia*.

Incorrect word	Lemma	Meaning	POS
arsa	arsa	said	V(PI)
clábar	clábar	mud	N(m)
choill	coill	forest	N(f)
bhia	bia	food	N(m)
lapadaíl	lapadaíl	paddling	N(m)
ó	ó	from	Prep.
rolladh	rolladh	roll	N(m)
anall	anall	back	Adv.
anonn	anonn	over	Adv.
mhuc	muc	pig	N(f)

Table 3: Top 10 words incorrectly selected as ciphers

5.4 Analysis of student texts

There were 184 sentences entered by the players. In order to encourage players to enter text and to avoid frustration at spelling errors in their own texts, a spelling checker feature was removed from this part of *Cipher: Faoi Gheasa*. This meant that the students could enter text of any kind - correct Irish, incorrect Irish, text in English or even nonsense text. An initial analysis of the players' texts indicates that there was actually quite a low percentage of texts (16%) that were in Irish and relevant to the story. The most common type of text was in Irish but not relevant to the story (39%), while 18% was Irish junk text. Texts in English accounted for 16% of the texts entered while nonsense junk comprised 14% of the texts. Table 4 shows the breakdown of texts by category.

Text Type	%
Irish - not relevant to the story	39%
Irish - nonsense	18%
Irish - relevant to the story	16%
Nonsense	14%
English	13%

Table 4: Analysis of students' texts by type

5.5 Corpus

The players of *Cipher: Faoi Gheasa* are contributing to a corpus of Irish learner texts. This corpus will continue to grow as more users play the game. While the corpus is currently small, it does provide a starting point for future research and will provide insights for Irish language educators, particularly primary school teachers and teacher educators. Millour and Fort (2020) report on interesting approaches for a crowd sourcing approach for low resource language and there is potential to leverage some of their findings in future work in this area.

5.6 User Experience Study

The evaluation and user study were analysed from the aspect of gaming experience, learning experience, adaptivity and usability according to the four-dimension evaluation framework (Law and Sun, 2012). In a survey of primary school students who played the game (n=64), 62.5% of the participants were positive about learning Irish through the game, 57.8% said the game was easy to play and 59.4 percent of the participants were willing to read the stories in the game. The full details of the evaluation process and results can be found in the study (Xu et al., 2022), which focuses on the user experience study of *Cipher: Faoi Gheasa*.

6. Discussion

6.1 NLP Perspective

It is important to ensure the quality of the texts used in *Cipher: Faoi Gheasa*. It was helpful to have the Irish POS tagger (Uí Dhonnchadha and van Genabith, 2006) for tagging the Irish texts and analysing the players' Irish sentences, as well as for analysing the level of texts. *Gramadóir* (Scannell, 2007) is a useful tool for checking Irish texts for spelling and grammar errors. One of the motivations for using the game with students was to gain extra insights into their knowledge of Irish spellings and spelling errors. The Irish POS tagger was useful for identifying the POS categories of the ciphers detected, not detected and incorrectly detected by the players.

Many low-resourced languages will not have a POS tagger available to them. While it was helpful to have a tagger, for other less resourced languages, a linguist could manually tag specific texts with the relevant XML tags which could then be fed to the Cipher engine.

6.2 Student Feedback

Feedback from students on the use of *Cipher: Faoi Gheasa* was positive. Given that almost all of their learning of Irish comes from classroom activities and printed textbooks, it was not surprising that they enjoy playing the app. Positive comments included *"its better than learning in the classroom"*. Asked what they liked about the game, one student replied *"not having to learn irish out of books"*.
When developing a GWAP, it is important that the game dynamics work for the players. Students understood the cipher storyline and context ("*the storyline is great*").
Some sample comments from students indicate that they really enjoyed the game.

> *"this game is very good and fun it is also very very entertaining we would rather do irish on this app than from [name] book thank you very much"*
>
> *"i think its a fun game and i would like if we could play it school. It is very adventurous."*
>
> *"the joy in winning the astonishing game"*

Learner autonomy is a feature of *Cipher: Faoi Gheasa* and students can play at their own pace. More advanced students will move through the game quicker while other students can move at a slower pace. Learner autonomy is advocated by Sanacore (2007) as a way of motivating reluctant learners and it is interesting to see that some players themselves were able to articulate this: "*the fredom and i prefer to play games than just get told things*".
While players could just scan the texts looking for ciphers, based on some student comments, it is interesting to see that some students did read the texts and understand the stories. One player commented that "*the witch died, which is what we wanted to happen*".
Students studying Irish have very limited exposure to Irish outside of the classroom (Harris et al 2006, cited in Hickey & Stenson, 2011). While Irish reading is not the sole focus of *Cipher: Faoi Gheasa*, it does provide a novel and interesting way for the students to read Irish texts. Students would generally only see Irish in a textbook, which can be a bit staid for some learners. The digital format particularly appeals to some students.
Another feature of *Cipher: Faoi Gheasa* is that students can write sentences in Irish as part of the game. They would generally not write texts in a digital format in Irish so this is a novel feature for them. One additional point to note about the use of *Cipher: Faoi Gheasa* in the classroom context is that even students who are exempt from studying Irish showed an interest in the game. This is particularly satisfying as often these students can feel excluded from class when the teacher is teaching Irish as they are assigned other tasks to do instead of Irish. This is a positive unintended consequence of *Cipher: Faoi Gheasa* - a more inclusive approach to teaching Irish.

7. Future Work

The NLP aspects of *Cipher: Faoi Gheasa* worked well but there is room for improvement in terms of some of the game dynamics. One student commented that they were not able to save their progress ("*no way to save your progress*"). However, there is a way to save progress and this will be made more obvious to players in future. Some students wanted extra pizazz in the game ("no *cool celebration*"). There were also issues to do with wifi connections and slightly old laptops which are obviously outside of the control of the developers but are issues that cannot be ignored nonetheless.

> *good game,but need more up to date laptop*
>
> *The game was kinda boring the hints dident help .... but it is very fun to play in school with your friends but it was ok nice game rate it a 5*

There is also a need to test *Cipher: Faoi Gheasa* with different types of schools. The players reported on in this paper were all from an English medium primary school (which make up the vast majority of Irish schools). It will be interesting to test *Cipher: Faoi Gheasa* with students from Irish-medium schools and also with students in Irish speaking regions of Ireland. *Cipher: Faoi Gheasa* could be suitable for adult learners as well and it will be tested with this cohort as well. We also intend to provide more texts in *Cipher: Faoi Gheasa* and to add new ciphers to the game. Also, it would be good to adapt *Cipher: Faoi Gheasa* to cater for the needs of A1 (complete beginner) students.

8. Conclusion

The development of Cipher: Faoi Gheasa was greatly facilitated by the use of the Cipher engine. The use of NLP tools and resources strengthened the game as they provided relevant information on parts of speech and enabled texts to be classified into suitable levels for learners. They also helped to ensure the quality of the texts presented to the players by identifying incorrect spellings in the texts at the preprocessing stages before they were provided to the Cipher engine. Students who have played the game reported that they enjoyed it and would like to continue to play it. This is encouraging as usually students will try to minimise the time they spend in class learning Irish. While developing NLP enhanced DGBLL apps for Less Resourced languages is more challenging, it is not impossible. This paper demonstrates that a structured and creative use of existing Irish NLP resources and generic NLP tools can be used to good effect to develop games that are pedagogically suitable and appropriate for language learners.

9. Acknowledgements

This work was conducted with the financial support of the Science Foundation Ireland Centre for Research Training in Digitally-Enhanced Reality (d-real) under Grant No. 18/CRT/6224. For the purpose of Open Access, the author has applied a CC BY public copyright licence to any Author Accepted Manuscript version arising from this submission. We would also like to express our special thanks to Tianlong Huang, who provided support for game development.

10. Bibliographical References

Blanco, C. (2021, December 13). The 2021 Duolingo Language Report. Duolingo Blog. Retrieved April 14, 2022, from https://blog.duolingo.com/2021-duolingo-language-report/

Breen, M. (1987). Leaner contribution to task design. In. C. Candlin& D Murphy. Language Learning Tasks. Englewood Cliffs, NJ: Pearson Prentice Hall.

British Council. (2014) English in Numbers. English in numbers | British Council. (n.d.). Retrieved April 14, 2022, from https://www.britishcouncil.cn/en/EnglishGreat/numbers

Central Statistics Office [CSO]. (2016). Census of population 2016–profile 10 education, skills and the Irish Language.

Chen, M. H., Tseng, W. T., & Hsiao, T. Y. (2018). The effectiveness of digital game-based vocabulary learning: A framework-based view of meta-analysis. British Journal of Educational Technology, 49(1), 69-77.

Council of Europe. (2022). The CEFR Levels. Common European Framework of Reference for Languages (CEFR). (n.d.). Retrieved April 14, 2022, from https://www.coe.int/en/web/common-european-framework-reference-languages/level-descriptions

Dixon, D. H., Dixon, T., & Jordan, E. (2022). Second language (L2) gains through digital game-based language learning (DGBLL): A meta-analysis. Language Learning & Technology, 26(1), 1-25.

Dunkel, P. (1991). Computer Assisted Language Learning and Testing Newbury House.

Gee, James Paul (2005) "Pleasure, Learning, Video, Games, and Life: the projective stance" E-Learning Vol 2, number 3.

Harris, J., Forde, P., Archer, P., Nic Fhearaile, S., & O'Gorman, M. (2006). Irish in primary schools: Long-term national trends in achievement. Dublin: Department of Education and Science.
Harvard

Hickey, T. & Stenson, N. 2011. Irish orthography: what do teachers and learners need to know about it, and why? Language, Culture and Curriculum, 24, 23-46.

Kincaid, J., Fishburne, R., Rogers, R. & Choissom, B. 1975. Derivation of new readability formulas (automated readability index, fog count, and flesch reading ease formula) for Navy enlisted personnel. Research Branch Report 8–75.

Law, E. L. C., & Sun, X. (2012). Evaluating user experience of adaptive digital educational games with Activity Theory. International journal of human-computer studies, 70(7), 478-497.

Millour, A., & Fort, K. (2020, May). Text Corpora and the Challenge of Newly Written Languages. In 1st Joint SLTU and CCURL Workshop (SLTU-CCURL 2020).

Millour, A., Araneta, M. G., Konjik, I. L., Raffone, A., Pilatte, Y. A., & Fort, K. (2019, May). Katana and Grand Guru: a Game of the Lost Words. In 9th Language & Technology Conference: Human Language Technologies as a Challenge for Computer Science and Linguistics (LTC'19).

Napier, K., & Whiskeyjack, L. (2021). wahkotowin: Reconnecting to the Spirit of nêhiyawêwin (Cree Language). *Engaged Scholar Journal: Community-Engaged Research, Teaching and Learning*, *7*(1), 1-24.

O'Brien, C. (2022, March 23). Inspectors concerned over quality of teaching, learning in Irish. The Irish Times. Retrieved April 14, 2022, from https://www.irishtimes.com/news/education/inspectors-concerned-over-quality-of-teaching-learning-in-irish-1.4834184

Oxford, R. L. (2006). Task-based language teaching and learning: An overview. Asian EFL Journal, 8(3).

Prabhu, N. S. (1987). Second language pedagogy (Vol. 20). Oxford: Oxford University Press.

Protheroe, N. 2004. Research report: Motivating reluctant learners. Principal 84 (1): 46–48.

Purgina, M., Mozgovoy, M., & Ward, M. (2017). MALL with WordBricks–building correct sentences brick by brick. CALL in a climate of change: adapting to turbulent global conditions–short papers from EUROCALL, 254-259.

Reinhardt, J. (2019). Gameful second and foreign language teaching and learning: Theory, research, and practice. Palgrave Macmillan.

Sanacore, J. (2007). Needed: Critics of literacy education with a more inclusive perspective. *International journal of progressive education*, *3*(1), 29-43.

Schmidt, R. (1992). Awareness and second language acquisition. Annual review of applied linguistics, 13, 206-226.

Sørensen, B. H., & Meyer, B. (2007). Serious Games in language learning and teaching-a theoretical perspective. In DiGRA Conference (pp. 559-566).

Tsai, Y. L., & Tsai, C. C. (2018). Digital game-based second-language vocabulary learning and conditions of research designs: A meta-analysis study. Computers & Education, 125, 345-357.

Uí Dhonnchadha, E. & Van Genabith, J. A Part-of-speech tagger for Irish using Finite-State Morphology and Constraint Grammar Disambiguation. LREC 2006, May 2006 2006 Genoa

Underwood, J. H. (1987) "Artificial Intelligence and CALL" in Modern Media in Foreign Language Education: Theory and Implementation. National Textbook Company.

Von Ahn, L. (2006). Games with a purpose. Computer, 39(6), 92-94.

Vygotsky, L. S. (1978). Mind in Society: the Development of Higher Psychological Processes. Cambridge, MA:

Ward, M. (2015). CALL and Less Commonly Taught Languages: Challenges and Opportunities. Research-publishing. net.

Ward, M. (2017). ICALL's relevance to CALL. CALL in a climate of change: adapting to turbulent global conditions–short papers from EUROCALL, 328.

Ward, M. (2019). Joining the blocks together–an NLP pipeline for CALL development. CALL and complexity, 397.

Ward, M., Mozgovoy, M., & Purgina, M. (2019). Can WordBricks make learning Irish more engaging for students?. International Journal of Game-Based Learning (IJGBL), 9(2), 20-39.

Xu, L., & Chamberlain, J. (2020). Cipher: a prototype game-with-a-purpose for detecting errors in text. In Workshop on Games and Natural Language Processing (pp. 17-25).

Xu, L., Uí Dhonnchadha, E., and Ward, M., (2022). User Experience Study of "Cipher: Faoi Gheasa", A Digital Educational Game for Language Learning and Student Engagement. In ACM GameSys'22, Athlone, Ireland.

Proceedings of the 9th Games and Natural Language Processing Workshop @LREC2022, pages 49–53
Marseille, 25 June 2022

The "Actors Challenge" Project

Collecting data on intonation profiles via a web game

Natallia Chaiko, Sia Vosh Sepanta and Roberto Zamparelli
CIMEC, University of Trento
name.surname@unitn.it

Abstract

This paper describes "Actors Challenge", a soon-to-go-public web game where the players alternate in the double role of actors and judges of other players' acted-out utterances, and in the process create an oral data set of prosodic contours that can disambiguate textually identical utterances in different contexts. The game is undergoing alpha testing and should be deployed within a few months. We discuss the need, the core mechanism and the challenges ahead.

Keywords: GWAP, prosody, Web games, NLP

1. Introduction

The study of intonation is an important part of semantic research, as it affects information structure, speaker's attitudes, structural ambiguity resolution and other syntactic and semantic phenomena. While there are now various well-established ways to annotate prosodic features (Pierrehumbert and Hirschberg, 1990; Gussenhoven, 2002) and tools to facilitate the annotation (see the recent ProsoBeast developed by (Gerazov and Wagner, 2021)), the exact mapping between prosodic features and semantics is not a solved problem, as is the consistency of such mapping across speakers and languages. While interesting attempts at a compositional theory of meaning/intonation have been done (see especially (Steedman, 2014; Schlöder and Lascarides, 2020)), they appear to be fairly language-specific, and do not consider the interaction between information structure and emotion. Similarly, some of the current research on the left-periphery of the sentence (devoted to (contrastive) topics and focus, question intonation, etc., e.g. (Frascarelli, 2010; Bianchi and Frascarelli, 2010)) rely on subtle prosodic cues which have not been verified by large pools of speakers, and whose consistency may be difficult to evaluate.

On another front, the study of emotions has been increasingly gaining attention due to its direct application to AI. In particular, comparative research across languages and cultures in word meanings, among them emotion words, has revealed interesting results and common patterns (see e.g. (Thompson et al., 2020)). Consequently, interest in data sets that revolve around emotions in speech has been steadily on the rise. One of the most recent ones, multilingual as well as multimodal, is the CMU-MOSEAS data set with over 40K labeled sentences (Bagher Zadeh et al., 2020). Once again, although the utterances are labeled according to the type of emotion they try to convey, the prosodic patterns are not annotated.

All of this research could profit from a large, multilingual, multi-speaker data set which reliably associates intonations and meanings in a controlled set of cases. To the best of our knowledge, a data set of this sort does not yet exists. The project closest to the one described in this proposal is the Mozilla-funded project Common Voice (Ardila et al., 2020), where volunteer speakers read sentences in their own languages and evaluate sentences read by others. The data set thus collected has broad language coverage (76 languages) and many hours of speech (about 2K validated hours just for English). However, sentences are presented and evaluated out of context, so there is no mapping between intonation and semantics beyond what can be extracted from the short passage to be read. A single sentence may be read differently by different speakers, but these differences cannot be traced to different discourse-level effects associated with them, or to the emotions the speaker intended to convey. There is also no incentive for careful validation, and no check to make sure that sentences are validated by speakers of the same variety, or even the same language.

2. Proposal

To address these gaps, and building on the experience gained from the oral data collection project VinKo, we propose a social web game, Actors Challenge (AC), designed to collect and validate large amounts of data on the correspondence between the intonation of a linguistic expression and its meaning in context. The success of projects such as DALI, on anaphora annotation (Poesio et al., 2013) and other linguistic data collection (Kicikoglu et al., 2020), has convinced us that intonation is a domain that could be appropriate for a 'serious game' design, administered over the web and mobile-friendly. This would also make it easy to deploy the game in multiple languages, so as to collect data comparable with materials from more traditional oral data repositories (e.g. VoxForge). Our plan is to initially launch the website interface and contents in English and Italian. After analyzing the pattern of usage and refining the materials, we plan to add German and Farsi, with ultimate goal of seeking out the collaboration of linguists abroad and expand the project to various other languages.

The basic setup (which draws from a method attributed to the Stanislavski's acting method by Roman Jakobson) (Jakobson, 1960) runs as follows.

- The researcher produces a linguistic expression, the *target*, which should be chosen to be very general (i.e. something that could be uttered in many different contexts, like *good evening*, *that's right*) and to be phonetically well distinguishable (to facilitate spectrographic analysis). Ideally, the target should be text that can also be easily adapted to different languages.
- The researchers then create a set of textual *discriminating contexts* in which the target could be uttered. Contexts, which could precede or follow the target, could be either the sentences adjacent to it (*John, boring Mary to death??* target = *Bill spoke to her for the whole evening*), or explicit descriptions of the circumstances in which it should be uttered ("You have just discovered a thief under your bed, and you say..." target = *Good evening*) or just bare stage directions (e.g. [*with affectation / with bitterness / pensive*]).
- The target's contexts give the background to understand how the target should be uttered, setting up the informational focus of the utterance, providing contrast or triggering different intonational profiles on the basis of their emotional content (i.e. surprise, fear, disgust, hurry, affection, hesitation, irony, etc.).

On the gaming side, the web site aims to attract players by offering them the opportunity to challenge each other on their 'active' and 'passive' acting skills: how much meaning and expression they can convey with their voice alone, and how fine-grained their understanding of other players' vocal nuances is. The mechanism works as follows.

The players log in into a web site, fill out a questionnaire (language and variety they identify with, gender, age) and are assigned to one of two roles: *audition* or *evaluation (casting)*. In the first one, they play the role of an actor that auditions for a part; in the second, they evaluate other players' performances and decide whether they correspond to a given context; the entire process is anonymous both ways. More specifically:

- In the *audition mode* the participant sees a (randomly chosen) written target sentence and a set of text-boxes containing the contexts (see Fig. 1). The participant selects one of the contexts, and records his/her voice uttering the target, aiming to implement the intonation that he or she feels appropriate for the context selected. The participant can listen to his/her recording, verify voice and recording quality, approve it if satisfied or repeat the recording. The auditioner then selects a different context, and repeats until all the contexts have a recording. The target is the same for all the contexts so, crucially, only the prosody can distinguish one from the other.

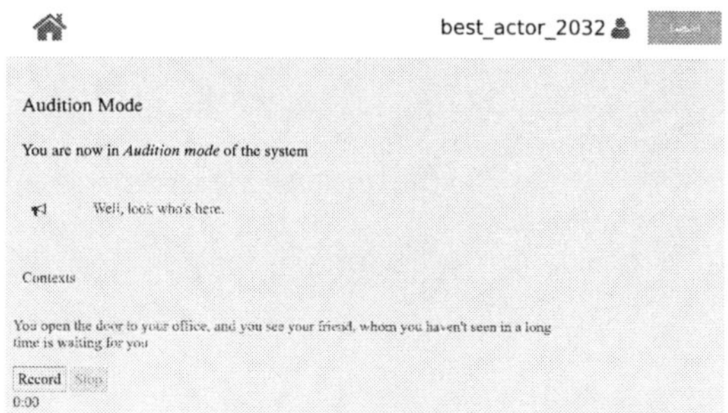

Figure 1: Detail of an Audition page screenshot.

- In the *evaluation mode*, the participant moves to a page with a set of contexts and a single loudspeaker icon (see Fig 2). Clicking on the icon, the evaluator hears a target that has been recorded by another participant in the auditioner role, and sees the set of contexts that was presented to the actor (in random order). The task is now to guess the context for which that intonation was meant. After the choice is done, the evaluator assigns a score to 'how convincing/natural' the performance was for the context chosen, using a 1–5 Likert scale (*performance rating*).

  A "Signal abuses" button is available at this stage to remove audios that have low sound quality, do not match the intended sentence, contain inappropriate contents, or add cues to facilitate context identification. These info can be used to alert the player and can trigger removal of the utterance and/or player.
- After a certain number of trials in one role participants are forced to do the other role, so as to maintain a balance.
- The primary measure of how good that intonational profile was at discriminating the semantics provided by the contexts — and thus how good an actor its utterer was — is the success rate of the evaluators in matching the recorded target with the context intended by the person who uttered it. A secondary measure is the 1-5 rating given to the performance by the evaluators. This is considered only if the attribution of the target to a context matches the intended context. Suppose, for instance, that player alpha had to utter "That's good." in four contexts A, B, C, and D. The player's utterance for context B is sent to 10 evaluators, 7 of which correctly assign it to context B, 1 to context A and 2 to C. The average rat-

ing assigned to alpha's utterance by the 7 evaluators who correctly classified it as meant for B contributes to alpha's score, along with the 7-out-of-10 proportion. The final score is given by the results for each of alpha's utterances (i.e. also those meant for contexts A, C and D).

- Players are also scored in their role as evaluators (the 'passive' side of acting). In this case the score is given by the variance of their judgments with respect to other evaluators' judgments on a set of cases for which there is a high level of correct identification. Scoring the evaluator's role should help increase the players' motivation in a task that could be perceived as less entertaining.

  When the performances of the participants have been judged by a sufficient number of evaluators, their *acting* and *evaluator scores* gets posted on a scoreboard. The players then receive an email from the system with an invitation to check their scores on the website and play again in the challenge.

- The acting scores will be organized in tiers, each linked to the names of famous actors. We will consider implementing the idea, suggested to us by an anonymous reviewer, that the acting score drops with time when left unused, as well as the possibility that advanced players gain the possibility of suggesting new contexts and targets for others to play. Taken together, these measures should motivate the players to return regularly to the site.

- From the researcher's viewpoint, intonation patterns which are consistently matched to a certain context and which have good ratings count as *validated data*: sound files with intonations which express a certain semantic content. The researcher also receives *negative* data: which intonation patterns are systematically associated to the wrong context, and which semantic contexts systematically fail to be disambiguated by intonations.

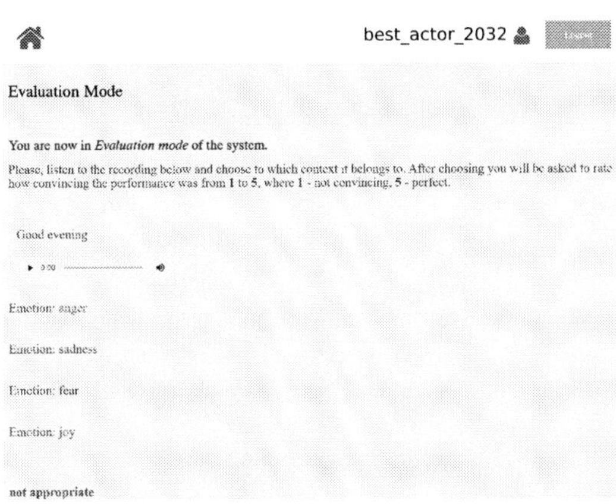

Figure 2: Detail of an Evaluation page screenshot.

3. Research targets

The outcome of the collection process described above would be a large set of intonations for the same linguistic expressions, along with the context or contexts to which they have been consistently associated (possibly, this could be distilled into a set of semantic features associated with that context, derived via crowdsourcing or via distributional semantic techniques). This material can be used for a variety of purposes, some of which require the possibility of automatic phonetic analyses of large amounts of data (but data with largely invariant lexical content). With the help of colleagues with an expertise in prosody and the meaning-intonation interface, we intend to look at the following topics.

- Examining the effect of combining multiple intonational patterns (e.g. question+surprise, question+emotion, multiple emotions). The compositionality of emotions is currenly an active research topic, but is mostly focused on bodily/facial features (see e.g. (Cavicchio et al., 2018)). The combination of emotions in speech, on the other hand, is an area that is relatively new and could benefit from a data set such as the one created by our AC project.
- Speech Emotion Recognition (SER): In the past 10 years the CL community has been busy developing models that would recognize emotion in spoken language (see (Yoon et al., 2018)); an essential factor in the effectiveness of these models is the data they are being trained on. We believe AC could contribute to building up this corpus.
- Examining how the intonation patterns varies from speaker to speaker. Inter-speaker variation is actively studied in labs (Niebuhr et al., 2011; Myrberg, 2013; Feldhausen, 2016) but not with the large volume of data that a web game could be expected to gather. Aspect to consider for investigation include irony, the difference between rhetorical and non-rhetorical questions, the theme/rheme distinction and the resolution of structural ambiguity. The amount of data allowed by a GWAP approach could also make possible to study the interactions among these phenomena.
- Examining how the intonation patterns vary across languages for the same semantic cues (translations of the same targets/contexts)
- Discovering ambiguous intonational patterns (i.e. targets consistently assigned to multiple contexts) and ordering semantic/emotion context w.r.t. how hard it is to consistently translate them into unambiguous prosody.
- Discovering the individual extent to which passive prosodic competence differs from active one (i.e. to what extent one can be a good evaluator without being a good actor and vice versa)

- Testing to what extent evaluators can correctly classify performances from actors from different parts of the country, and possibly even different languages. Note that normally evaluators will be asked to evaluate the performances of people in the same area, obviously excluding one's own performance.
- Probing the ability of players to recognize other players' individual *voices*. This data will be gathered by adding a yes/no question to the evaluation mode: "Do you think you have heard the voice of this actor before?". Comparing the answer to the history of auditioners the player has encountered gives us the ground truth.

Beyond this specific research questions, we believe that the data collected with a game, if successful, can be extremely valuable to training general computational models of intonation, both in production and in perception. All the data collected, anonymized in conformity to the EU GDPR policy, will be made available to the public under a Creative Commons BY-SA 4.0 license. Last but not least, we will explore the idea of using this data as an ingredient in the creation of distributional multi-modal meaning representations of emotion terms, associating e.g. "fear" to the set of intonations that people use to render fear contexts.

.

4. Avoiding caricatures, removing abuse

One possible drawback of the Actors Challenge design is that, based as it is on discrimination, it might lead to non-natural, exaggerated utterances. For instance, if all I have to do is to say *tonight* as a question or an assertion I might simply exaggerate the raising intonation in the question, creating an unnatural, 'caricature' question. In other terms, focusing on context discriminability rather than prosodic appropriateness makes the actors adapt their intonation only to the specific set of contexts, as it might happen for the target in the two set (1) (worrying/nonworrying) and (2) (worrying/scary).

(1) TARGET: Who are you?

a. **Context 1**: it's late at night and you are alone in the office. Someone knocks at the door, but you do not expect anyone. You open. It is big man, with a scar and a strange smile.

b. **Context 2**: it's late at night and you are alone in the office. Someone knocks at the door. A young girl with a sweet smile stands there, a little embarrassed.

(2) TARGET: Who are you?

a. **Context 1**: it's late at night and you are alone in the office. Someone knocks at the door, but you do not expect anyone. You open. It is big man, with a scar and a strange smile. = *(1-a)*

b. **Context 2**: it's late at night and you are alone in the office. Someone knocks at the door. It's a green, humanoid monster with a large toothed mouth.

At the data-gathering level, the presence of caricatural intonation could sometimes be a feature, not a bug, as it might be used to better highlight prosodic differences. However, it would certainly be inappropriate for other uses of the data (AI model training). To contain the damage, we plan to employ the following features:

- Using the *Performance score*: beside assigning the utterance to a context, the evaluator assigns a score to it. With appropriate instructions ("Rate how natural the utterance sounds in this context") this can be used to penalize caricatural answers. The auditioners are made aware of the fact that the rating is part of their scores.
- A higher number of alternative contexts (currently 4) should make the problem less pronounced, since with many contexts it would be too difficult to contrastively tailor intonations.
- Another possibility to explore is to tell the performer that at evaluation time multiple performances assigned to the same context in different auditions will be randomized. In other terms, the evaluator might be given the context set in (2), but the utterance to evaluate could sometimes be the one the actor has associated to (1-a), rather than (2-a).

As in any distributed data gathering exercise, our game presents a trade-off between sound quality (with poor recordings due to low quality microphones, noise, speaker's volume or other factors) and amount of data (Lafourcade et al., 2015). The possibility for the actors to listen back to his/her own utterance before submitting it should partly address this, as could the shared experience as evaluators, which would raise the participant's awareness of the importance of good sound. Using the game on mobile devices could also help, since cellphones' microphones are often better than PC's and the actors are likely to speak closer to the mike; noise will worsen going mobile, but there are good tools to clean up this aspect at data-preparation time. Evaluators have a button to raise alarm about the poor sound quality of specific utterances, and repeated alerts are fed back to the players at log in.

Another concern is the possibility of abuse. This could take the form of completely inappropriate recordings (e.g. insulting remarks replacing the target) or attempts to conditions the outcome by adding information above and beyond the intonation. To counter this possibility, the evaluators have a "Signal abuse" button. Multiple abuse alerts on one utterance lead to exclusion of that utterance from further evaluation. Repeated cases lead the system to (temporarily or permanently) ban players. We will also experiment with dictation software to double check if the utterance matches the target.

5. The current state of the project and its future

The software engine for the audition/evaluation has been developed in Java by one of the authors and is ready to be deployed, modulo minor feature addition. The front-end of the website is currently under revision, with the goal of giving it a more refined, game-like look and making it suitable for mobile devices. The next step will be to adapt the new interface to the engine. After these steps, the site will be open to beta testers by summer 2022. If this phase is successful, we plan to advertise it among a limited circle of users, whose feedback will help us fine-tune the game (materials, feedback parameters, interface) and improve interactive features, like the scoreboards. We will then advertise it on social media and start the real data-gathering exercise. In parallel, we will be expanding our set of contexts and languages (currently only English and Italian), and translating the interface (currently only in English). As mentioned above, the contexts include textual descriptions of the circumstances in which the target is uttered, including emotion cues and focus. Researchers interested in using our tool could provide further targets and contexts in the form of a spreadsheet. We will however work hard to make sure that the game contains enough playful material to keep the players entertained: "serious games" should never be as serious as labs.

6. References

Ardila, R., Branson, M., Davis, K., Henretty, M., Kohler, M., Meyer, J., Morais, R., Saunders, L., Tyers, F. M., , and Weber, G. (2020). Common voice: A massively-multilingual speech corpus. In *Proceedings of LREC*.

Bagher Zadeh, A., Cao, Y., Hessner, S., Liang, P. P., Poria, S., and Morency, L.-P. (2020). CMU-MOSEAS: A multimodal language dataset for Spanish, Portuguese, German and French. In *Proceedings of the 2020 Conference on Empirical Methods in Natural Language Processing (EMNLP)*, pages 1801–1812, Online, November. Association for Computational Linguistics.

Bianchi, V. and Frascarelli, M. (2010). Is topic a root phenomenon? *Iberia: An International Journal of Theoretical Linguistics*, 2(1).

Cavicchio, F., Dachkovsky, S., Leemor, L., Shamay-Tsoory, S., and Sandler, W. (2018). Compositionality in the language of emotion. *PloS one*, 13(8):e0201970.

Feldhausen, I. (2016). Inter-speaker variation, optimality theory, and the prosody of clitic left-dislocations in spanish. *Probus*, 28(2):293–333.

Frascarelli, M. (2010). Narrow focus, clefting and predicate inversion. *Lingua*, 120(9):2121–2147.

Gerazov, B. and Wagner, M. (2021). Prosobeast prosody annotation tool.

Gussenhoven, C. (2002). Intonation and interpretation: Phonetics and phonology. In *Speech Prosody 2002, International Conference*.

Jakobson, R. (1960). Linguistics and poetics. In T. Sebeok, editor, *Style in Language*, pages 350–377. Massachusetts Institute of Technology Press, Cambridge, MA.

Kicikoglu, O. D., Bartle, R., Chamberlain, J., Paun, S., and Poesio, M. (2020). Aggregation driven progression system for GWAPs. In *Workshop on Games and Natural Language Processing*, pages 79–84, Marseille, France, May. European Language Resources Association.

Lafourcade, M., Joubert, A., and Le Brun, N. (2015). *Games with a Purpose (GWAPs)*. (Focus Series in Cognitive Science and Knowledge Management). John Wiley & Sons.

Myrberg, S. (2013). Sisterhood in prosodic branching. *Phonology*, 30(1):73–124.

Niebuhr, O., D'Imperio, M., Fivela, B. G., and Cangemi, F. (2011). Are there "shapers" and "aligners"? individual differences in signalling pitch accent category. In *17th ICPhS*, pages 120–123, Hong Kong.

Pierrehumbert, J. and Hirschberg, J. (1990). The meaning of intonational contours in the interpretation of discourse. In P. Cohen, et al., editors, *Intentions in Communication*, pages 271–312. MIT Press, Cambridge, Mass.

Poesio, M., Chamberlain, J., Kruschwitz, U., Robaldo, L., and Ducceschi, L. (2013). Phrase detectives: Utilizing collective intelligence for internet-scale language resource creation. *ACM Trans. Interact. Intell. Syst.*, 3(1):3:1–3:44, April.

Schlöder, J. J. and Lascarides, A. (2020). Understanding focus: Pitch, placement and coherence. *Semantics and Pragmatics*, 1(13).

Steedman, M. (2014). The surface-compositional semantics of english intonation. *Language*, 90(1):2–57.

Thompson, B., Roberts, S. G., and Lupyan, G. (2020). Cultural influences on word meanings revealed through large-scale semantic alignment. *Nature Human Behaviour*, 4(10):1029–1038.

Yoon, S., Byun, S., and Jung, K. (2018). Multimodal speech emotion recognition using audio and text.

Proceedings of the 9th Games and Natural Language Processing Workshop @LREC2022, pages 54–60
Marseille, 25 June 2022

Generating Descriptive and Rules-Adhering Spells for Dungeons & Dragons Fifth Edition

Pax Newman, Yudong Liu
Western Washington University
516 High Street, Bellingham, WA, USA
{newmanp, liuy2}@wwu.edu

Abstract

We examine the task of generating unique content for the spell system of the tabletop role-playing game *Dungeons and Dragons Fifth Edition* using several generative language models. Due to the descriptive nature of the game, it presents a number of interesting avenues for generation and analysis of text. In particular, the "spell" system of the game has interesting and unique characteristics as it is primarily made up of high level and descriptive text but has many of the game's main rules embedded with that text. Thus, we examine the capabilities of several models on the task of generating new content for this game, evaluating the performance through the use of both score-based methods and a survey on the best performing model to determine how the generated content conforms to the rules of the game and how well they might be used in the game.

Keywords: Generative Language Models, Game Content Generation, Dungeons & Dragons

1. Introduction

Dungeons and Dragons (D&D) [1] is a tabletop role-playing game (RPG) that boasts a large player base across the world and features a wide and detailed set of rules. It is also a game which encourages creativity and offers its players a great deal of freedom in play. In this work we are using the Fifth Edition version of the game, as it's currently the newest and most popular version of the game.

1.1. The Game

The gameplay of D&D revolves around the interaction between two groups to simulate a story taking place in a fictional world, where one group attempts to perform actions in this world and the other determines what happens when those actions take place. This back-and-forth gameplay is supported by a set of rules that gives participants a guideline how to resolve the actions and events that take place in the game. The two groups consist of a player known as the dungeon master (DM), and the rest of the participants who are referred to as players. The DM holds a position that is equal parts referee and storyteller. They are responsible for describing and simulating the world of the game for the players. Since the game has a freeform nature to it, the DM also has the responsibility of determining how to enforce or use the rules when players attempt to do something outside of the usual purview of the rules. On the other side, the players hold a relatively simple position of taking the role of characters within the world of the game and, as a player's respective character, interacting with the world that the DM describes for them. Since the DM is responsible for what occurs in the game, they also determine what, if any, extra non-official content to allow players to use. As such, a DM will tend to only allow non-official content into their game if they deem it to be fair for use. In this context, "fair" generally means that it is not so powerful or useful that it makes the game too easy or invalidates other content. In addition, for players whose primary job is to act as their character, some don't feel that the officially provided content offers enough options and will often seek content created by a third party so that the abilities of their character might better match what they envision.

1.2. Spells

One facet of D&D is its spell system, which allows players to use magical abilities during gameplay to enact some action on a being or object in the game. Every spell has eight parts, with many of them being highly dependent on others. Table 1 shows an example of spells in D&D. As seen in the table, these parts are the *title*, *level*, *components*, *casting time*, *range*, *duration*, *school*, and *description*. For this work we focus on the *title*, *range*, *duration*, and *description* as they carry the most importance to how a spell functions during gameplay. The descriptions of spells have a high variance in content, function, and length. They also have the most impact on how a spell works and what it does. Some spells have very simple descriptions that describe a single function the spell performs; others have long descriptions detailing a more complex spell that could be used in many ways. Descriptions also feature narrative language of what occurs when a character in the game casts the spell. No matter what a spell is though, every description has information about broader rules of the game embedded within it through the use of keywords and phrases.

1.3. Motivation

Due to the distinctive qualities of these pieces of text which hold both narrative and rules-oriented language

[1] https://dnd.wizards.com/what-is-dnd

Title	Phantasmal Killer
Level	4th
Components	Verbal, Somatic
Casting Time	1 Action
Range	120 ft
Duration	Concentration, 1 Minute
School	Illusion
Description	You tap into the nightmares of a creature you can see within range and create an illusory manifestation of its deepest fears, visible only to that creature. The target must make a Wisdom saving throw. On a failed save, the target becomes frightened for the duration. At the end of each of the target's turns before the spell ends, the target must succeed on a Wisdom saving throw or take 4d10 psychic damage. On a successful save, the spell ends. At Higher Levels. When you cast this spell using a spell slot of 5th level or higher, the damage increases by 1d10 for each slot level above 4th

Table 1: An example of official spells

in them, we see this as a unique type of text for the task of natural language generation. Showing that modern language models have the capability to infer rules from text and generate new content while retaining a narrative style of language is an interesting and unique task that could have broader impacts in the field. In addition, the use of natural language generation in the field of tabletop role-playing games could be a powerful tool. Since these games are based primarily around the use of written and spoken language, they could be enhanced through the use of computer generated content used before or during play to generate content for specific scenarios as the need arises. With this work we also hope to bring to light some of the unique facets of TRPGs as a medium that hold potential for future work in content generation and player interaction. (Liapis et al., 2014) presents the many interesting features of video games when it comes to the topic of computational creativity. We believe TRPGs to hold many of the same features as video games in this field, as well as other features unique to this medium.

2. Related Work

There is plenty of work in automatic text generation for video game content and character dialogue (Côté et al., 2018; Urbanek et al., 2019; Sirota et al., 2019; Ammanabrolu et al., 2020; Liu et al., 2021; Yao et al., 2020; Walton, 2020). One of the most related works to ours is (Woolf, 2019) on generating cards for the game *Magic the Gathering*[2] This work utilized a generative language model for generating cards and is like our work in that the cards contain descriptions similar to the descriptions of D&D spells but without the descriptive language. In their work they fine-tuned GPT-2 (Radford et al., 2019) to generate certain parts of a card by inserting unique marks on the parts of interest, such as using brackets around one component or parentheses around another. We adapt a similar technique to tag each part of a spell's data with the hope that the models would learn to differentiate each component and how they relate. It also serves as a convenient technique for checking which parts of a spell have been generated by examining the tags.

Besides this work, there are other works that are not quite as closely related, but still highly relevant. For instance, *AI Dungeon 2*, which utilizes the GPT-2 1.5B parameter model to generate "choose your own story" style adventure games. This model has been deployed online[3] with much success and shows the possibilities of using these sorts of models as a core gameplay mechanic.

(Ammanabrolu et al., 2019) presents methods for using a Markov Chain model and a Neural Language Model to generate game content. They use models to generate content in the form of quests that provide a player with a set of objectives to complete towards some goal. These quests center around players being given a list of ingredients and a recipe they must complete. The neural model in this work utilizes an LSTM (Hochreiter and Schmidhuber, 1997) model to generate a list of ingredients, which is then fed to GPT-2 to generate a title and a set of instructions to complete based on the ingredients. This work incorporates a human-participant study to determine a number of qualities of these quests, such as their coherence and creativity, as well as if the player felt accomplished upon completing them. This work is highly related to our own as both attempt to generate textual game content that needs to be coherent and creative through the use of a neural language model.

(Fan et al., 2020) presents a work on using machine learning (ML) algorithms to compose worlds for a text based game. In this work, worlds are described as being made up of various locations connecting with one another, with each location containing characters and objects that a player can interact with and use. The authors use multitask learning to train several models to connect pre-made locations together to make the world, populate the world with characters, and populate the world with objects. In addition to using ML to construct and populate worlds, they employ a transformer based model to generate new characters and objects which can then be placed into the newly generated

[2]https://magic.wizards.com/

[3]https://play.aidungeon.io/

<namestart> Acid Splash<nameend> <rangestart>60 Feet<rangeend> <durationstart>Instantaneous<durationend> <descriptionstart>You hurl a bubble of acid. Choose one creature within range, or choose two creatures within range that are within 5 feet of each other. A target must succeed on a Dexterity saving throw or take 1d6 acid damage. At Higher Levels. This spell's damage increases by 1d6 when you reach 5th level (2d6), 11th level (3d6), and 17th level (4d6).<descriptionend>

Table 2: An example of the training dataset

world.

3. Approach

Our approach to this work involves the following four components: 1) Create a viable dataset; 2) Train several generative models on the data; 3) Compare each model's performance using scoring metrics BLEU and BERTScore and subjective analysis of the quality of text generated; 4) Lastly, take spells from the best performing model and incorporate them, alongside human-made spells, in a survey given to players of D&D to determine player desirability and consistency with the rules. The models we decided to use for generation are an N-Gram model using Markov Chains, a model utilizing LSTM layers, and GPT-2 by OpenAI fine-tuned on our dataset.

4. Dataset

We used a collection of all 554 official D&D spells[4], as well as 2,598 player-made spells from the website `http://dandwiki.com`. For the player-made spells we had to create a web scraper to gather the relevant data. We then combined both datasets into a single file and removed all data irrelevant to the work such as a spell's school or components. The text for each spell then contained its *title*, *range*, *duration*, and *description*. We tagged each spell's attributes using tags such as "<namestart>" and "<nameend>" and concatenated all the attributes of a spell together into a string. We then removed 50 randomly picked spells from the entire dataset to be used later for evaluation. This left us with 3012 spells in our training set. Table 2 shows an example of our training dataset.

5. Experiments

5.1. N-Gram

Our N-gram model is a simple word-based 6-gram model that was trained with no smoothing. The training data for this model was unique from the others. The input data was not tagged but instead we placed "signifiers" such as "*title:* " and "*description:* " before each spell attribute. We then concatenated the spell attributes into a single string for each spell and used this as the training data for our model. In addition, each string was padded with tags for the beginning and end of the spell. During generation we truncate everything generated after the end tag if it has been generated.

5.2. LSTM

Based on common practice, the LSTM model we used is a standard character-based model that contains an embedding layer with dimension of 256, two LSTM layers of size 1024 and 512, respectively, dropout layers after each LSTM layer with a dropout-rate of 0.1, and lastly a dense layer the size of the vocabulary. Our vocabulary for this model contains 48 characters in total (all alphanumeric characters, in addition to 12 punctuations and symbols including !, ?, ;, :. ', ", (,), -, +, <, and >). This model was implemented using the Keras library[5]. We trained it on 200-character long sequences from our dataset for over 100 epochs and with a learning rate of 0.001. The data for this model was slightly altered, as each spell also contained tags to indicate the start and end of the spell. During generation we truncated everything generated after the end tag if it has been generated.

5.3. GPT-2

Our GPT-2 model was implemented with HuggingFace's transformers library[6]. We fine-tuned the pretrained model offered by the library on a text file that contained every spell in our training dataset. This fine-tuning took place over 3 epochs. Our training data for this model was slightly different as we combined the tagged text for every spell into a single text file which was then given to the model. We did not use tags to signify the start and end of a spell for this model. However, during generation, we did truncate everything generated after the first tag signifying the end of a spell's description was generated.

6. Evaluation

Our evaluation contained three parts, a baseline examination using BLEU scores, an examination with BERTScore, and a survey with our best model, the GPT-2 based model.

6.1. BLEU Score

BLEU scores (Papineni et al., 2002) are generated based on the average number of overlapping one, two, three, and four-grams between a "reference" sentence and a "hypothesis" sentence. For our evaluation, we generate a hypothesis sentence by taking the first 40 tokens of a reference sentence and using that to generate the hypothesis. Since the LSTM based model uses

[4]https://www.kaggle.com/code/josephstreifel/dnd-spells/data

[5]https://keras.io

[6]https://huggingface.co

characters rather than word tokens, we use the first 200 characters of a reference sentence to generate the hypothesis. Each hypothesis is then compared to its reference sentence and all of the scores and average to find the final score of the model. We chose this as a baseline scoring metric as it's widely used in quickly measuring the quality of generated text compared to some reference text and is easy to understand and interpret.

6.2. BERTScore

BERTScore (Zhang et al., 2019) is used to measure similarity between two sentences by leveraging BERT's contextual embeddings to calculate the cosine similarity between each token in a reference sentence to each token in a predicted sentence. For this part of the evaluation we use the same reference and hypothesis sentences described above for the BLEU scores. We chose this as a scoring metric as it can more accurately capture the semantic similarity between two sentences than more naive approaches like BLEU, which is relevant for our work as there could be many ways to word a spell and have a similar result. We used the implementation provided by HuggingFace's Datasets library.

6.3. Survey

For our final evaluation we created a survey containing 5 GPT-2-made spells that we determined to be good results, and 5 randomly selected player created spells for D&D from `https://www.dandwiki.com/wiki/`. Without labeling where the spells were from and with random ordering, we asked respondents the following questions for each spell:

- "*What do you think made this?*"
- "*How well do you think this spell conforms to D&D's rules?*"
- "*Would you play/allow this spell?*"

Each of these questions were multiple choice. The first had options of "*Human*", "*AI*", and "*I've seen this spell before, and I know it was made by a human.*". The second was a choice from 1 to 5 with 1 being "*Doesn't fit in with the rules at all*", and 5 being "*would fit in right alongside official spells*". The third was also a choice from 1 to 5 with 1 being "*Definitely wouldn't*" and 5 being "*Definitely would*". The survey was posted in several D&D focused Discord servers including one for a D&D club at our institution.

7. Results

7.1. BLEU Score Results

The BLEU score results in Table 3 show that there's a much higher number of n-gram overlaps between the reference and generated spells for GPT-2 than both other models. This may indicate that GPT-2 more often uses the same words and phrases in the reference spells. Since BLEU penalizes generations that are shorter than their reference, it's worth mentioning GPT-2's tendency to generate long repetitions of text which may have pushed the results partially in its favor. However, since the other two models also occasionally had generations that were very long, we suspect GPT-2's habit of repetition did not skew the results and that the relative scores are still accurate.

Model	BLEU Score
N-Gram	6.6
LSTM	10.7
GPT-2	17.7

Table 3: BLEU score results for each model

Model	Precision	Recall	F1
N-Gram	0.756	0.852	0.801
LSTM	0.886	0.891	0.888
GPT-2	0.932	0.914	0.923

Table 4: BERTScore results for each model

7.2. BERTScore Results

The BERTScore results in Table 4 show that the semantic similarity of spells generated by GPT-2 is higher than those generated by the other models. Since the hypothesis spells were generated with only the first 40 tokens of the reference sentence, they were generated largely based off of the *title*, *range*, *duration*, and a small piece of the *description*. Due to this, the scores would indicate that the meaning and wording of the generated description is closely related to that of its reference spell's description. It's worth mentioning that unlike the other models, GPT-2's precision is higher than its recall. This indicates that many tokens generated by GPT-2 are closely related to some set of tokens in the reference spell, but not as many tokens in the reference are in that set and thus have few similar counterparts in the generated spell. This could be due to GPT-2 being pre-trained and thus having the capability to generate words that aren't in our dataset.
In addition, general observation of the spells generated by each model such as those in Table 5 demonstrates the level of ability of each model. A reading of the example from GPT-2 indicates that spells generated by GPT-2 are capable of a high level of coherence and the descriptions contain similar patterns and wording as seen in official spells. Due to the high level of performance of GPT-2 compared to the other models, we chose only spells generated by GPT-2 for use in the survey.

7.3. Survey Results

A total of 14 people responded to the survey, and all of them identified as people who play D&D. With a sample size as small as 14 responses, it's hard to glean any true conclusions from our survey. However, as you can see the results are extremely close in all categories. D&D players were successfully able to identify an AI

Model	Spell
N-Gram	Title: fire whip Duration: concentration, up to 1 hour Range: touch Description: when you cast this spell using a spell slot of 3rd level or higher, 30 seconds are added to the time the target is banished for each slot level above 4th. the creatures must be within 30 feet of each other when you target them.
LSTM	Title: Projectile Creature Range: 10 feet Duration: Instantaneous Description: A Warlice distortion of your hands in your fanging prowess, as a bonus action on a location within range you entered. Happiness points that are instantaneously runlois pit functions, along with its quantity of the caster or the caster such as metal weight.
GPT-2	Title: Magical Blade Range: 10 feet Duration: Instantaneous Description: You create a magical blade which resembles a blade of magical force. Choose a creature within range. Each creature in a 20-foot-radius sphere centered on that creature must make a Strength saving throw. On a failed save, a creature takes 5d10 force damage and is knocked prone. On a successful save, the creature takes half as much damage. At Higher Levels. When you cast this spell using a spell slot of 4th level or higher, the damage increases by 1d10 for each slot level above 3rd.

Table 5: Example spells generated by each model

	Player Made	GPT-2
Correctly Identified	57%	59%
Average Rule Conformity	3.39	3.37
Average Playability	3.47	3.49

Table 6: Survey results

generated spell slightly more than the human ones, while the AI spells were reported to conform to the D&D rules slightly less yet be slightly more playable with more respondents saying they would use/allow these spells in their games. It's also worth noting that for one AI generated spell, 2 of the 14 respondents claimed to have seen the spell before and knew for a fact it was written by a human. No other spell got this response, and it's clear the respondents hadn't seen that spell previously. We suspect that due to the simplistic nature and brevity of the spell, these respondents recognized common traits between it and other similar spells they had seen before. Given the small differences between the corresponding survey scores between human-made and GPT-2-made spells, it appears that our generated spells are of similar quality as the spells from `https://www.dandwiki.com/wiki/`.

Title	Conjure Ray of Force
Range	Self
Duration	Instantaneous
Description	You channel the power of your spirit into the ray of force and create a ray of force that is stronger than the spell's damage. The ray of force deals an extra 1d8 force damage to all targets within range. Target one creature in range. On a hit, the target takes 1d8 force damage. This additional damage is increased by 1d8 if you cast the spell at the same time every day for the past 24 hours.

Table 7: One example of problematic generation from GPT-2

8. Error Analysis

Although the spells were received relatively well by the survey participants, there are a number of problems in the spells generated by GPT-2.

The spell in Table 7 is evidence of generation that shows interesting and novel generation in the sentence, "*This additional damage is increased by 1d8 if you cast the spell at the same time every day for the past 24 hours*". This introduces a mechanic that could be interesting in play. This mechanic however is not well used in this spell, and would be better used in a spell that is unrelated to combat. In this way the model succeeds in utilizing an interesting mechanic, but fails to use it in a way that enhances the spell.

As for the spell in Table 8, its description is fine and works well on its own, however it's entirely inconsistent with the spell's range and duration. In the description it states "*You create a bolt of thunder that flies from your hand towards a willing target. Make a ranged spell attack against the target*", however the range of the spell is "*Self*". This sort of contradiction is a common problem with spells generated by this model and commonly occurs with each attribute of the spell. For example in this spell this type of problem occurs with each attribute of the spell and its description.

Title	Step into Darkness
Range	Self
Duration	1 Minute
Description	You create a bolt of thunder that flies from your hand towards a willing target. Make a ranged spell attack against the target. On a hit, the target takes 3d6 lightning damage. On a miss, the target takes half as much damage.

Table 8: Another example of problematic generation from GPT-2

9. Conclusions and Future Work

9.1. Conclusions

In this work, we explored to use 3 generative language models for automatic spell generation for the game D&D. Our results show that language models can generate texts at a comparable level to amateur designers, with descriptions that are both thematically interesting and fitting to the set of rules inferred by the text in the training corpus. This technique could be applied to other aspects of D&D or other games to generate new and interesting content. This could be used in many ways, such as an aid for designers creating new content for a game where a model might generate several suggestions to what the designer is currently writing, similar to modern email and messaging clients giving generated suggestions. Since tabletop games like D&D require extensive planning on the part of the DM, a system to generate new content for them could dramatically reduce the work required to prepare content to play the game, thus making it easier for more people to play and enjoy the game.

Generating new content in this manner could also be used during gameplay either to supplement gameplay or as a deliberate mechanic by the game's designers. This could lead to an entirely new kind of tabletop game where the content is generated dynamically as the game progresses.

9.2. Future Work

As this work is still a preliminary exploration in this field, there are several places for improvement upon both our best model and the others. The first place of improvement would be finding more data, and the second place would be pre-processing the data further. Since many of the spells used for training were sourced without regard for any sense of quality, there were likely biases and problematic sections that the models learned. Removing some of these problematic spells would be a step in the right direction for improving results. However, simply obtaining more data could resolve the issues presented by problematic spells, as the model would likely have more good spells to learn from in a larger dataset. Having a wider array of spells in the training set would also be highly beneficial, as each of the models tend to only generate spells that deal damage.

One potential method to deal with the bias towards damage-oriented spells would be to split the data apart into spells that are primarily damage focused and those that aren't, and train or fine-tune a model using each of these sets separately. This may be a good method to make up for the large differences in the two types of spells.

Using a more powerful model such as larger and more powerful versions of GPT-2 or newer architectures like GPT-3 could also yield significant gains. Since these spells can sometimes have very long descriptions that need to remember key information during the entire generation, such as the title or range, it would be useful to use a more powerful model that has a better ability to retain information.

Overall there are many places in which this task could be improved to create even better results than the already considerable ones shown here.

In summary, this work shows that modern generative language models can be a potentially powerful tool to aid the design and play of tabletop roleplaying games like D&D and any other games that rely on descriptive text that is embedded with rules.

10. Bibliographical References

Ammanabrolu, P., Broniec, W., Mueller, A., Paul, J., and Riedl, M. O. (2019). Toward automated quest generation in text-adventure games. *arXiv preprint arXiv:1909.06283*.

Ammanabrolu, P., Cheung, W., Tu, D., Broniec, W., and Riedl, M. (2020). Bringing stories alive: Generating interactive fiction worlds. In *Proceedings of the AAAI Conference on Artificial Intelligence and Interactive Digital Entertainment*, volume 16, pages 3–9.

Côté, M.-A., Kádár, A., Yuan, X., Kybartas, B., Barnes, T., Fine, E., Moore, J., Hausknecht, M., Asri, L. E., Adada, M., et al. (2018). Textworld: A learning environment for text-based games. In *Workshop on Computer Games*, pages 41–75. Springer.

Fan, A., Urbanek, J., Ringshia, P., Dinan, E., Qian, E., Karamcheti, S., Prabhumoye, S., Kiela, D., Rocktaschel, T., Szlam, A., et al. (2020). Generating interactive worlds with text. In *Proceedings of the AAAI Conference on Artificial Intelligence*, volume 34, pages 1693–1700.

Hochreiter, S. and Schmidhuber, J. (1997). Long short-term memory. *Neural computation*, 9(8):1735–1780.

Liapis, A., Yannakakis, G. N., and Togelius, J. (2014). Computational game creativity. In *ICCC*.

Liu, J., Snodgrass, S., Khalifa, A., Risi, S., Yannakakis, G. N., and Togelius, J. (2021). Deep learning for procedural content generation. *Neural Computing and Applications*, 33(1):19–37.

Papineni, K., Roukos, S., Ward, T., and Zhu, W.-J. (2002). Bleu: a method for automatic evaluation of machine translation. In *Proceedings of the 40th annual meeting of the Association for Computational Linguistics*, pages 311–318.

Radford, A., Wu, J., Child, R., Luan, D., Amodei, D., Sutskever, I., et al. (2019). Language models are unsupervised multitask learners. *OpenAI blog*, 1(8):9.

Sirota, J., Bulitko, V., Brown, M. R., and Hernandez, S. P. (2019). Towards procedurally generated languages for non-playable characters in video games. In *2019 IEEE Conference on Games (CoG)*, pages 1–4. IEEE.

Urbanek, J., Fan, A., Karamcheti, S., Jain, S., Humeau, S., Dinan, E., Rocktäschel, T., Kiela, D., Szlam, A., and Weston, J. (2019). Learning to speak and act in a fantasy text adventure game. *arXiv preprint arXiv:1903.03094*.

Walton, N. (2020). Ai dungeon 2: creating infinitely generated text adventures with deep learning language models.

Woolf, M. (2019). How to make custom ai-generated text with gpt-2, Sep.

Yao, S., Rao, R., Hausknecht, M., and Narasimhan, K. (2020). Keep calm and explore: Language models for action generation in text-based games. *arXiv preprint arXiv:2010.02903*.

Zhang, T., Kishore, V., Wu, F., Weinberger, K. Q., and Artzi, Y. (2019). Bertscore: Evaluating text generation with bert. *arXiv preprint arXiv:1904.09675*.

Author Index

Association for Computational Linguistics
209 N. Eighth Street
Stroudsburg, Pennsylvania 18360

ISBN 978-1-7138-6121-8
9 781713 861218